FAMILIARITY IS THE KINGDOM OF THE LOST

Dugmore Boetie was essentially a con man. The facts of his life were for ever changing, constantly being amended, altered and updated and inevitably conflicting with one another. But if Dugmore Boetie hadn't been a con man, he would probably never have had either the daring nor the imagination to write, to translate the events and fantasies of his life into so vibrant and honest an expression of anger, hope and despair.

From the first page, when Duggie pushes his mother into the fire, the extraordinary magic-lantern show of Boetie's life never slackens pace. He moves from a job in the circus, washing the feet of the elephants, and sleeping in the backs of buses, to living in the sewers while picking pockets, stealing, suffering the filth and brutality of the Bantu prisons and finding and losing a wife. There seems little hope for a one-legged, unemployed, black ex-convict with an incriminating pass book. But it is Dugmore Boetie who has the last laugh.

Dugmore Boetie died in 1966.

Barney Simon, now Artistic Director of the Market Theatre Company in Johannesburg, worked closely with Dugmore Boetie on his manuscript and was responsible for its first publication in 1969. Among many other texts he has created with actors is the highly acclaimed *Woza Albert!*, which he brought with remarkable success to London's West End.

FAMILIARITY IS THE KINGDOM OF THE LOST

FAMILIARITY IS THE KINGDOM OF THE LOST

By Dugmore Boetie
Edited by Barney Simon

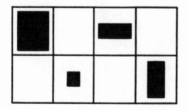

Four Walls Eight Windows, New York

First U.S. paperback edition published by:
Four Walls Eight Windows
PO Box 548
Village Station
New York, N.Y. 10014

First printing April 1989.

Library of Congress Cataloging-in-Publication Data:

Boetie, Dugmore.
Familiarity is the kingdom of the lost/by Dugmore Boetie;
edited by Barney Simon.—1st U.S. paperback ed.
p.   cm.
ISBN: 0-941423-20-4: $6.95
1. Boetie, Dugmore. 2. Crime and criminals—South Africa—Biography.
I. Simon, Barney. II. Title.
HV6248.B645A3 1989
364.1'092'4—dc19   89-1568
[B]   CIP

FAMILIARITY IS THE KINGDOM OF THE LOST

I

'Say "*mother*"! Go on, say "*mother*", you son of a bitch!'

Wham! Wham! went the leather strap.

'Say "*mother*", damn you! Louder, you little bastard, louder!' she shrieked.

The strap went wild all over my face, head, and neck. It was as if she was suffering more than me.

My mouth opened, and instead of the word 'mother' a clot of blood rolled out. It was followed by a distinct '*Futsek!*' She shrieked and swung a frying pan, cracking four of my ribs. I pushed and her skinny body fell to the greedy flames of a healthy fire-galley.

Maybe I had broken her back, or maybe she was just too exhausted to lift herself. Anyway, my mother just fried and fried and fried. . . .

'Where is he?'

'We've got him in bed thirteen.'

'How is he?'

'Oh, his ribs are coming on fine and we took the stitches out of his right thigh this morning. It's the cut above his eye that seems to worry him. He'll soon be out of here.'

'You're a social worker, aren't you?'

'Yes, Nurse.'

'I wonder how old he is?'

'Between seven and eight, I'd say.'

'God,' said the nurse.

'What's going to happen to him when he gets out of here?'

They were many now, all ringed around my bed discussing me as if I had fallen from heaven and had broken a wing. The one not in uniform shrugged her shoulders and said:

'These cases are many; they might be different, but the pattern is the same. Take this one – he's too young to be sent to a

7

reformatory and too old to be placed in a crèche. Children of the gods above and the gutters below. One day, with God's help, the Government will build a home for them.'

My ribs were not fully healed when I ran away from hospital. I walked back to Sophiatown where I got myself a job at the Good Street bus depot. It was more voluntary than fixed.

I worked without asking permission from anybody. I busied myself sweeping stationary buses with an improvised rag broom.

At night, I would wait for the last bus to come in. It had to be the last bus because you never knew which one might pull out first. The last bus would come in between eleven thirty and twelve midnight and then I'd coil myself on the back seat and sleep.

When the first bus pulled out at four a.m. I would get up and stand at the corner of Good Street and Main Road to wait for the baker's horse-cart. Right on time I would hear the clop-clop echoes of the horses' hoofs on the tar road as they galloped towards Newlands. This was a daily routine. They were delivering fresh-baked bread to the white inhabitants of Newlands.

I would stand hidden behind one of the shop pillars and watch the driver till I was sure that all his attention was centred on the road before him, then I would dart swiftly out of my hiding place and without hesitation jump lightly on the back step of the van. Sometimes I would just sit there with my bare feet dangling while I enjoyed the ride.

One morning I was too hungry to brag. I pulled at the thick wire loop to swing the door open, but nothing happened. Then I noticed that the van was freshly painted. The paint made it difficult for me to lift the loop; it needed stronger hands. Hands that materialised right out of the tar road. Or so it seemed. One minute I was struggling with the wire loop and the next I knew, a different pair of hands appeared mysteriously and lifted the loop without effort.

'Jump!' was all he said.

I did. We retreated up Main Road with four loaves of fresh-baked bread under our armpits. When we came to the spot where he had so mysteriously appeared, he stopped and eyed me speculatively.

8

'Where's your home, boy?'

I shook my head. 'No home.'

'Where d'you sleep?'

'At the bus depot in Good Street, on the back seat of the last bus.'

He had a big dent in his forehead and it was throbbing violently as if it was inhaling and exhaling. He was very much undecided about something. What made him come to a quick decision was the shouting we heard from the still-receding baker's cart.

We had forgotten to close the back door of the van. The door was flapping wildly in the wind and someone was hailing the driver, hoping to draw his attention.

'In here,' said my new-found father. He threw himself on to his stomach and, sliding crabwise, vanished into the gutter.

I was still undecided when I felt his fingers closing around my ankle in a powerful grip. That decided me. I went flat on my stomach and slid in after him.

I felt him crawl, and I followed. We had crawled for only a few yards when suddenly he wasn't in front of me anymore. If he hadn't grabbed me, I would have blundered head-first into a larger tunnel.

Here it was blacker than the inside of a devil's horn. You couldn't see your own hand in front of you, but at least you could stand upright.

'Follow me, and trail with your hand against the wall,' he said.

I did. We travelled this way for about a mile, and then we stopped. He groped for my hand and led me up four steps. Up here, he was forced to stoop, while I still remained upright.

That was how I first met the man who was responsible for my future life. It was a dog's life, but nevertheless a life.

I heard him going through his pockets, then I heard the rattle of matches. He struck one. The flame nearly blinded me. He got a lamp from somewhere, and lit the wick.

I gasped. I was looking at the cavern of Ali Baba and the forty thieves. Only that was fiction and this was real.

The walls were plastered with pictures of Tom Mix the cowboy. Strewn on the floor was what must have come fresh from a washing line. There were bed-sheets, pillow-cases, ladies' bloomers, men's underwear – all were still damp. There was a

9

wheelbarrow, a gramophone and records, a stale wedding-cake, a police helmet, a pressure stove, pots, a red battered money-box, a guitar with three strings, and a horseshoe nailed to the entrance to keep away evil spirits.

But above all the prizes, my eyes kept straying towards the gramophone. He must have noticed this, because he went straight to it and started playing some records.

I looked around and saw that this part of the tunnel was V-shaped. Water couldn't come through here because he had placed a thick slab of cement to block the outlet that runs through to the main tunnel. One tunnel was then forced to share the water of the other. What really helped a great deal was that we were about three feet above the major tunnel.

After enjoying some of the records, we had our breakfast. Then my father started schooling me on the numerous small tunnels that start in and around Sophiatown and end up here in the big one.

I was taught when and how to take advantage of them, which one to use, and which one to avoid, where they led to, and what to do in case of rain. It was like a game of snakes and ladders with the ladders crossed out. We didn't need the ladders because they led up. All we needed was the snakes. The snakes swallowed us, and when we crawled out of their bowels we found ourselves back in our underground home with arms heavily laden with stolen goods. And no tail behind.

I looked with awe at my father when he was through explaining. He was an unusually short man. Because of this, it was difficult to determine his age. He could have been anything between twenty and forty.

He told me that his real name was Ga-ga, but because of his bandy legs, people referred to him as Kromie, 'Crooked' in Afrikaans. When I begged him for permission to refer to him as Ga-ga, which was his real name, meaning not to remind him of his bandy legs, he refused. He told me that in the American comic strips ga-ga means mad; he wasn't mad.

The dent in his forehead was frightening to look at. It was so big that you could fit a tennis ball into it. He told me that it was caused by the hoof of a farmer's horse. I started hating horses until this very day.

Kromie was bad through and through. He was more mischievous than troublesome. He could without effort cause a highly religious person to use vile words. Wherever he went he left grief and chaos behind. I honestly don't think that he could walk past a dry field of grass without setting fire to it. His pocket money came from children sent to the shops by their parents. My teaming up with him did not improve my relationship with the young population of Sophiatown nor the Main Road shop owners. There was a verbal prize hanging on our heads.

Take Honest Charley, for instance, from the Chinaman shop next to the bioscope. He was named Honest Charley instead of Black Market Charley. This Chinaman kept a big pocket watch in one of his waistcoat pockets. The man was attached to a chain.

I must have made a note of it unconsciously. One morning, after oversleeping and missing my usual bread supply on the road, I went into the shop to buy myself a tickey's worth of bread. I was suddenly struck by a mischievous brainwave.

'Charley,' I said, leaving out the Honest part of his name, and holding out the bread in my hand, 'will you please push this bread down the back of my neck? I'm afraid the other boys will snatch it and run into the bioscope with it.' Charley grinned, showing a row of golden teeth.

While Charley was busy pushing the bread down the back of my neck, I lifted the watch.

It was more through fate than anything else that I bumped into Ga-ga, my gutter father, as I was leaving the shop. Outside, I showed my father the watch. He whispered fiercely into my ear, then he dragged me back to the shop's entrance. He called to Charley who was busy scaling sugar into six-penny bags.

When Honest Charley looked up, Ga-ga said, 'Look, he's got your watch.' Honest Charley dropped what he was doing and grabbed a meat cleaver. If I had known that the watch meant so much to him, I wouldn't have pinched it. Maybe he had come all the way from Chinaland with it.

I wanted to run for my life, but Ga-ga held me fast. The cleaver was being brandished with murderous intent. I tried to pull free from Ga-ga, but he held on. It was only when the cleaver was lifted for the fatal blow that Ga-ga let go. I ran down Main Road as if the Devil was after me. Maybe he was, at that.

Then Ga-ga went into action. He darted into the empty shop, jumped over the counter, and emptied the till. . . .

I was lying flat on my stomach, another morning, with my cheeks resting on the palms of my dirty little hands. A gramophone record was playing.

The voice in the record belonged to Jimmy Rodgers. He was singing a song called 'Waiting for the Train' with guitar accompaniment. The first time I heard that record, I took to it like a drunkard takes to drink.

I must have been really dreaming. Of what? Only my ancestors know. But what I do know is that I was dreaming, because Kromie had looked up from his comic strip and said,

'I'm talking to you!'

'What?' I asked.

He pointed a fat jam-stained finger at the comic strip. 'Do you think the Red Indians will catch him?'

To shut him up I said, 'Yes, he doesn't stand a chance.'

My Daddy chuckled gleefully at the plight of the pony express rider. As long as you agreed with him, nothing went wrong. I didn't want anything to go wrong. Not while I was listening to that record.

But something did. Good things don't last. My father trampled on my favourite record by accident.

A nightmare search for the record started. Every time I stole a record, it would turn out to be the wrong one. You see, I couldn't read. If I could, I would have saved myself a lot of trouble and the Jew a lot of grief.

It went on so long, that I was beginning to think that the old Jew at the bicycle shop didn't have that record.

But my will was as obstinate as the cracks on my mud-caked feet. I was in and out of that Jew's shop as if I owned it. At last I got the right record and six months in the reformatory. The youngest convict there.

When I came out, I was bitterly reprimanded by my father for stealing records instead of food.

One morning I went out as usual for our daily bread. When I came back, the gramophone was missing. My father had sold it during my absence. He claimed that it was spoiling me.

I felt as though my back was broken. My bowels wanted to work. I packed my guitar and left the tunnel for good to wander again in a world of uncertainty.

I didn't wander long. I soon found myself working for a circus, washing elephants' feet. Sometimes I wondered which feet needed to be washed most, mine or the elephants'. But seeing that I wasn't getting paid to wash mine, I didn't bother with them.

I travelled with the circus to Cape Town where for the first time I saw the sea.

In Cape Town I was mostly with a Coon Carnival group known as The Jesters. There was a guitar player that I greatly admired. He played almost like my Jimmy Rodgers. We were inseparable; I trailed behind him like a devoted young pup.

He sent me everywhere. I went daily to town for him to pick up cigarette stubs and empty wine bottles. Eighty empty wine bottles landed him a full one at the liquor store. In turn he taught me a few chords on the guitar.

I was so busy running errands for my friend that the circus left without me. I didn't care much. I was fed-up with the elephants' feet and getting tips instead of wages. I felt that if I kept on washing elephants' feet I'd never get around to washing my own.

I liked Cape Town because sleeping accommodation was no problem. I just slept where I felt sleepy. In corridors. On stairs. Balconies. Anywhere. I just lived, and lived, and lived.

My life was so free that I was just beginning to be convinced that this nice town had no reformatory. Then they arrested me for trying to steal a bus conductor's money bag.

My knife was too blunt, otherwise I would have gotten away with it. I had his money bag, which was hanging from a leather strap, with my left hand, while my right was slashing at the leather strap which was buckled to the bag. The damn-fool knife wouldn't cut the strap in one stroke. The white conductor tried to grab my knife hand. That made me forget the leather strap. Instead, I sank my knife through his hand. It's funny, the knife wouldn't cut the strap but it sank through his hand as if it was made of reformatory soap. That got me two years in Tokai, the Cape Town reformatory. The kind of work they gave me in the reformatory got me out of the reformatory. We were weaving fishing-nets. My nimble fingers were so good at it that in a year they gave me a 'hat' as promotion. I was now a monitor.

It was while I was a monitor that I learned about the fish train. The fastest train on the track. It travels non-stop from Cape Town docks to Johannesburg, with one water break at Bloemfontein so that the fish it carries shouldn't get rotten. The non-stop journey plus the chunks of ice with which they line the coaches keep the fish still fresh all the way to Johannesburg.

Maybe the fishing-net business was beginning to bore me. Or perhaps it was the fish train knowledge. I don't know. All I know is that I found my hands manufacturing a rope ladder instead of a fishing net, while the corner of my right eye kept straying towards the prison walls. It's a long time ago, but I can still hear the echoes of police whistles in my ears whenever I recall what I now refer to as the Tokai Break. They behaved as if I was forty instead of eleven.

Seven days after my escape from Tokai, a policeman was saying,

'Jump over his head and get to the other side, then work on the fingers of his left hand while I work on the right.'

A crowd of onlookers had gathered on both sides of the fish train. I was perched between two coaches. The white policeman on my right was grumbling and swearing as he struggled to release my frozen fingers from the wire cage of the coach. He was hurting me. The other policeman on my left was more gentle.

'Can't we light a fire and melt the ice around the little devil's fingers?'

'No, he'll get frostbite.'

'I wonder how the devil the little bastard got himself into such a mess.'

He gave one quick unexpected pull and my right hand was jerked free. Blood dripped from my fingers and tears spurted from my eyes as I examined my bleeding hand. The nail on my little finger was missing.

'Better do the same with that left hand, we can't afford to waste any more time with this little brat.'

'Hold on, I'm only left with the thumb.'

Pulling the baton from his belt, he knocked it several times against the wire cage. The ice cracked and fell away, and my thumb was free.

They hauled me off the train. At first, my knees wouldn't let me stand upright, but after the police gave them a good rub I was able to stand unaided.

'Pikannin!'

'Yes, baas.'

I looked up at the policeman with a dirty, tear-stained face.

'What on earth were you doing on that train?'

'I was trying to get loose, baas.'

'Yes, yes, I know. What I don't know is how the hell you found yourself hemmed in between two coaches and half-frozen to death?'

'I was coming home, baas.'

'Coming home from where?'

'From Cape Town, baas.'

'You mean,' spluttered the other policeman, 'you travelled a thousand miles from Cape Town like that?'

'I come from Cape Town with this train, baas.'

'Where do you stay, boy?'

'Sophiatown, baas.'

'What street, boy?'

'Good Street, baas.'

'What number?'

'No number, baas.'

'You mean there is no number at your house?'

'No number, baas.'

'Why?'

'Is not a house, is a bus garage, baas.'

'You mean you sleep in a bus depot?'

'Yes, baas. On the back seat of the last bus.'

'The back seat of the last bus, heh?'

'Yes, baas.'

'This is a case for the social workers. . . .'

'Not social workers, please, baas.'

'Why not social workers?'

'Long time ago, they say I'm a head sore.'

'A what?'

'A head sore, baas.'

'You mean a headache?'

'Yes, baas.'

'How old are you?'

'Leben.'

'Eleven!' they echoed in unison.

As I was led through the gaping crowd, I fished out a half loaf of stale bread from inside my shirt and started biting into it.

I didn't care what they were going to do with me as long as I was back home. Familiarity is the kingdom of the lost.

They locked me up and only released me when they felt that I was old enough to look after myself. I could, too, if the police would only stop interfering.

2

After four years I was out.

A rasping kind of sound came from my new khaki prison suit as I walked away from the Auckland Park Reformatory towards Westdene. I drowned the monotonous sound by jingling the money that was in my pocket. Reformatory wages – two shillings a month for four years. Four pounds sixteen shillings.

My mind was dwelling on the parting words of our convict preacher: 'Son, once you come to the outside world, teach yourself to look upon problems as the wheels of progress. Go forward with them and you won't go wrong. Reverse, and you end up here.'

The people who preach most about reform are found in prison. When you're free, you wonder where the hell they are. When you go back, you find them there. You don't dare ask them why they didn't follow their own advice. They go on like a whore that tells every man in bed with her, in all seriousness, that she has never had it so good before.

Lying to yourself is the biggest sin of all because you end up the sufferer. Why fry your own carcass? Why stand in judgement on yourself? Clear your conscience by elbowing the blame. You have as much right on this earth as the next man. My advice is:

keep the blood-pumper out of it and give the reins to the brains. But in this country a hungry stomach takes the place of brains. Use it. Take or be taken. The home of the timid is the grave.

If you want to get rich quick, take the road that leads to prison. There's a steel door at the end. As you go to it, don't go in, turn sharp right. Then you're on your way.

I came to the first gate that led into Newclare Township. The gate I call 'Weaklings turn back'. Instead of making the sign of the cross because I was just about to enter into hell, I took out a bag of strong prison tobacco. It's a Xhosa tobacco commonly known as Ndanya Ndanya – 'I shit, I shit'.

Newclare Township lies five miles west of Johannesburg City. In those days it was an African township, encamped right round with an iron spiked fence. Whoever thought of that giant-size cage must have thought it proper to place the inhabitants of this township on the same level as wild animals; because in all my born days I've never seen a township frequented so much by police vans, except, perhaps, its opposite neighbour, Sophiatown.

There were four legal entrances to Newclare, each closely guarded by hefty Zulu policemen armed with heavy knobkerries. The knobs of their kerries were covered with spiked buttons of steel.

In spite of these security precautions, the rough elements of the township tampered with the iron fence that so jealously guarded them and you could always find man-size holes at convenient points.

The first entrance led directly into Ballendine Avenue. This was the only tarred street in the whole township because it led to the superintendent's home and office.

Turn right or left at any street you came to. If you were black, you'd see life. If you were white, life would see you.

The streets were divided by ox-cart-wide alleys. If you stopped at the mouth of any alley and shot a glance either way, you were sure to see the bent form of a woman hauling skokiaan from a drum that lay mouldering in the ground.

Right where you were, if you knew what to look for, you'd see someone, male or female, resembling part of the surrounding scenery.

Immediately after the skokiaan queen rose from her undig-

17

nified position and disappeared into one of the back yards, the inconspicuous figure would also disappear. There was nothing mysterious about this. The party just happened to be scouting for police while the skokiaan queen hauled her brew.

If you kept on along the avenue, you came to the tramlines and the football grounds. Then you turned right. You were at another gate, the second entrance to Newclare. The biggest and busiest of the township.

First thing that I looked for here was the gutter that led to the tunnel where I lived as a boy. Next, the 'Prisoners Corner' near the public lavatories. Here you'd see Africans – as many as fifty to a hundred – sitting miserably in a long queue. Closer inspection revealed that they were handcuffed in pairs. Pass-law victims.

The familiarity of such a scene hardly warranted a second glance, unless you wanted to invite enquiries about your own pass.

You turned your eyes away from those bundles of misery to the elderly women sitting in half-circles selling fried corn cobs. They worked over fire-galleys made out of four-gallon paraffin tins with holes punched into them. Some sold pork trotters and sheep trotters in pots blackened by wood and coal smoke. There were coffee carts where you could get a quick cup of coffee in the open or a shilling's worth of skokiaan on the sly. Some women sold hard-boiled eggs, and right next to them a Coloured woman also sold eggs. Hers went much faster because the insides contained brandy mixed with tobacco juice.

There was a little waiting-room built by the Johannesburg Municipality Transport Company to shelter tram passengers from the rain. The only patrons of this little waiting-room were a gang of unruly teenagers waiting to pick the pockets of passengers as loaded trams rumbled in from the city.

Written inside the waiting-room in bold red letters were the words: BENZINE GANG. Next to the waiting-room stood the skeleton of the township's only telephone booth, long since out of use.

I crossed Main Road and left Newclare to mingle with the pawns on the Devil's board – Sophiatown.

My beloved Sophiatown. The skeleton with the permanent

grin. A live carcass bloated with grief and happiness. Where decency was found in filth and beauty hidden behind ugliness. Where vice was a virtue and virtue a vice. A black heaven glowing with sparks of hell.

From its feverish womb crawled many of the country's finest black doctors, teachers, sportsmen, businessmen, musicians and intellectuals. Also its best-dressed criminals.

Sophiatown mothered all races. That's why her apron was always dirty. Without blushing she could produce a Timbuctoo Swahili with the same ease as she would a Zulu flat-boy. She looked upon them all with the equal affection of a long-suffering parent.

Here, four hundred miles inland from the nearest coastal town, American influence ran thick. Because Sophiatown was the first black town in the whole of Africa that could boast a cinema as far back as the early twenties. As civilisation advanced, so did the evil life of Sophiatown. I saw the turnover from the traditional stick fights to fist fights, and then to the buckles of heavy scout belts. From there, it was knives, and then guns. Sophiatown became a slum jungle of here-today-and-dead-tomorrow.

Just across the main road from Newclare was Good Street and the notorious and one and only bus-rank. Whoever named this street must still be wriggling in his grave. This street was no damn good. It was hell's own highway. Bad through and through. It was nearly impossible to go from one side to the other without paying a fine in broken ribs or a busted head.

Saturdays and Sunday afternoons were sheer hell. The Pedi gang used to have fist fights in shebeen backyards just to see which one of them was strong enough to lead the pack. Then they'd storm down Good Street towards the bus-rank, leaving pedestrians screaming and cursing as they painfully picked themselves up from the ground. A cyclone gone mad.

Then there were the Zulu gangs. Their undying belief is that they represent the bravest and strongest black race in the whole of Africa. Me, I think they are just plain stubborn. They would come in groups from the beer halls, waving and hitting the air with their heavy sticks, fighting an imaginary foe. Often the foe was not imaginary, especially when they reached the bus-rank at Good Street where they were sure to come face to face with the

19

Basutos. The result was always a free-for-all, with a few scattered dead and badly maimed bodies. Mostly Sothos.

The Sothos also moved about in groups. They wore cone-shaped straw hats, and bright blankets covered the top half of their bodies. Underneath those colourful blankets, they carried dangerous sticks. If you saw Sothos coming towards you in a group, you got the hell out of their way. Their way of fighting was first to cover the victim with their blankets and then to beat him to death. If they detected movement under the blanket, they justified their blood-thirsty act by suggesting that the victim was fighting back. If they hit you and you fell, they said you were picking up stones. If you screamed, you were calling your brothers to come and kill them.

Those were a few of the playmates you could find at the corner of Good Street and Main Road.

At night time it was even more jazzy. Then you could always meet up with true, cultured gentlemen like the Black Caps. They were a gang of more than fifty. Here's a typical operation: A man takes a stroll with his wife. He's smartly dressed in his own way – brown-and-white shoes, grey flannel trousers, black blazer, cream straw hat. The fool is swinging his wife's handbag like it's a briefcase. His bragging ways make the Black Caps jealous. So one of them says, 'Look at that romantic bastard. He must be a real black Clark Gable to be able to own such a beautiful brown doll.'

Then another one of them says, 'I'm going to show that bum that the fact that I don't own a cow doesn't mean that I don't like meat. He thinks it's only people with baskets that can go to market.'

So they strip him of his clothes and his wife. His wife he gets back the next day.

A little further up Good Street was the untidy bus depot where I made my first job and slept as a child. You were always sure to find a circle of men gathered on the pavement nearby shooting dice.

These gamblers were the real hard cases of Sophiatown. My reformatory wages needed increasing. I decided to go and try my luck. When my turn came to pick up the dice, I dropped a ten-shilling note and made my challenge. I bent half-forward and shook the dice, waiting for my challenge to be answered. I didn't wait long before four half-crowns came spinning down from above.

On my first throw, up came the winning number. It was number eleven. I reached out with my left hand to pick up the money, when I heard a voice growl. It was just that, nothing else; just a growl like an animal imitating speech.

I looked up. What I saw made me take a step back. The money was completely forgotten. In all my life I'd never seen such a frightening brute! His head was clean-shaven, showing many brutal scars that brought to mind bicycle chains, heavy belt buckles, knives, axes – you name it. What was fascinating was that there were no stitch marks on any of those swollen scars. They must have healed with no outside help. They looked like criss-cross pieces of rope.

He grinned at my blatant stare. That made him even uglier. He had a huge scar that started just above his left eye and ended below his chin. His lips were badly scarred too. Everything expanded when he smiled.

'Throw again,' he said. 'Can't you see the dice is not sitting straight?' He sounded like a leaking organ in B flat.

I gulped and picked up the dice again. It wasn't necessary to shake them because I was shaking already. I threw, and another winning number came up. This time it was number seven. As I reached for the money, the gorilla growled again.

I threw so many damned times that I felt my back ache. At last I threw a double six, a crap. The losing number. 'Aaah,' beamed the son-of-a-bitch. 'Now you lose.' With bile and disgust in my mouth, I threw the dice in the middle of the school and walked away.

I sat in the back yard of a Chinese grocer's shop drinking bath-tub brandy and related my grim crap game experience to some fellow drinkers. One of them looked at his friend and grinned as if enjoying a secret joke.

'This, my friend, is Sophiatown. Here you must look before you leap. Last night I was enjoying myself at a friend's party way up Gold Street. At eleven o'clock I took off my clothes until just my underwear was left. My friend asked why I was going to sleep so early when the party was just getting hot.

'"Sleep?" I said. "I'm not going to sleep – I'm going home!"

'"How the hell can you go home in your underpants?"

'"You wait and see," I said. They all thought I was drunk or mad.

'I opened the door and began to jog home at a nice dignified pace. Just when I came to the Newclare fence, I heard a voice coming from a dark shop doorway:

'"Leave that one alone. Can't you see they've already stripped him?"

'Hell, I smiled to myself. You see, I wouldn't have stood a dog's chance and I knew it. When I leave here, I'm going straight to my friend's place to collect my clothes.

'Yes, my friend, Sophiatown is becoming a real hell town. The police are not improving it either with their pass laws and their liquor laws. Now they have passed a new law known as "Lekker Loop". It's really "Drunken Noise". The fine was ten shillings or ten days. Now it's fifteen pounds or three months.

'Man, now they are arresting us left and right. Even if you're not drunk, they'll claim you *are* drunk! Day before yesterday, no! It was Monday morning at the corner of Victoria and Bertha Street, I found a white policeman arguing with an elderly man. The policeman said the man was drunk. The man said he was only on his way to work. "Then," said the policeman, "if you're not drunk, why the hell do you eat fish and chips in the street?"

'"I'm hungry, baas, that's why."

'The policeman clipped handcuffs on his wrists and said, "Come on, only drunkards eat in the street. Besides, you're shivering."

'As he was being led away, I heard the man say: "I'm shivering because I'm angry, not drunk."' The speaker sighed, then took another deep breath as though he was going to launch into a new yarn.

'Do you know this ugly ape who did me down there?' I interrupted quickly.

'That, my friend, is Number Nine. He is called that because of that ugly scar like a nine on his face. Keep well away from Nine, he's dangerous. He fights like hell, but what's so bloody unfair is that he doesn't seem to get hurt. Fighting him is like fighting grinning rubber!' Everyone nodded in agreement.

There and then I decided to spend all my reformatory wages on Nine. I'm going to make the son of a bitch drunk, I said to myself, and when he's nice and drunk, I'm going to beat him half to death. Either I get Nine, or he gets me.

3

It was either the bitter taste of bile in my mouth, or the stench seeping through the broken window of the latrine that woke me. Maybe it was both.

The taste of bile was so thick that I wouldn't have been surprised to see a purple face in the mirror. And Christ! did that lavatory smell! Imagine one bucket-latrine catering for a whole yard of people. It was being used inside and out. I needed to vomit.

I got out of the bed without studying my surroundings. I went straight to the water bucket without bothering to look for a mug. I picked up the four-gallon bucket and drank a quarter of its contents. I looked about for a basin and saw one. I didn't care what kind of basin it was – a dish-washing basin or a face-washing basin. I went down on my knees in front of it and pushed three of my fingers down my throat in the hope of drawing the bile out.

It worked. When I was through, the basin was filled with green stuff. It was as if some evil had just snaked out of me.

I took the basin out and emptied it in a blocked drain. I went back to the little room and sat on the only bed, my head resting between my hands. I was trying to review the events of the night before. Much as I tried, I couldn't recall a thing. Thinking only increased the pain in my head, so I gave it up and studied my immediate surroundings. There was nothing to study. The room was bare, except for two benches and the bed I was sitting on.

Suddenly I jerked upright as I thought of my reformatory wages. Hastily I ran through my pockets and uncovered four shillings. I went through them more carefully, emptying everything on the bed. Everything meant prison tobacco, matches, pieces of brown paper that I used for rolling the tobacco and

23

finally, my prison discharge papers. I looked at the brown pieces of paper, half willing them to turn into pounds, then the room turned dark. I looked up, and there was the large figure of Nine blocking the door.

He was grinning from ear to ear. Hell's chief stoker. Whatever decided me to try and fight that brute I'll never know. I had as much chance of winning as David would have had if he had fought Goliath fair.

'How you feel?'

'Never mind my feelings, where's my money?'

'You dranked it, Little Brother.'

'All?'

'You told the shebeen queen to decorate the table and count the empties.'

'Then what happened?'

'Drinks make you brave, Little Brother. When you were drunk you took a swing at me. I caught your fist over my shoulder and hanged your body there instead, then I carried you home.'

'Just like that, heh?'

'Just like that.' He grinned.

I groaned and fell across the bed. When I again looked up, Nine was busy cooking thick porridge on the pressure-stove. When the porridge was cooked, he produced a thick slice of beef steak. The steak was still dripping blood when it joined the porridge. I thought that surely somewhere the cow was still alive.

After feeding he said, 'How much money you got?'

Instead of telling him to go and shovel the bones in hell, I heard myself saying, 'Four shillings.'

'Gimme,' he said, just as rudely.

'On the bed,' I said listlessly. He took the money and left.

I lay back and stretched myself. I was unused to strong liquor, it was playing hell with my nerves. As for my four shillings, I didn't give a damn what was going to happen to them. I had just made the painful discovery that I was incompetent to look after myself. I was here to serve humanity. My gutter father. Then the circus population. Then the Coon Carnival guitarist. Then the reformatory authorities. Now Number Nine.

The worst feeling was inside me. A depressed feeling of human oppression that caused my insides to shake like raw eggs, leaving me mentally, physically and spiritually in a funk. A frightening feeling of self-pity, the foundation of disaster.

I must have slept, because when I came back to the world without pity, the sun was just going down in the west.

I got up and lit the piece of candle that was perched on the bottom of an empty jam tin. Its feeble light revealed bloody stripes of long-dead bed bugs on all four walls. I closed my eyes again.

'Wake up, Little Brother,' came the hateful voice. 'It's Christmas for you and me. Your four shillings got me eight pounds – three for you, and five for me.'

He threw the money on the bed and grinned. I wished that he wouldn't grin so much. Somehow, that grin made me feel lost, like I was intruding in a man's world. It made the reformatory look like a much safer place.

'Put on your jacket, Little Brother, we're going out tonight. First, we're going to Sisinyana's shebeen where we'll drink a few mugs of skokiaan until the clock strikes twelve. That's when our lives will begin, Little Brother, at midnight.'

As we crossed the deserted main road of Sophiatown, I saw someone lying in the middle of it. I told Nine. I wish I hadn't.

'Let's go and see, Little Brother. This is going to be a lucky night.' I followed reluctantly. Nine turned the still form over. The man was covered with blood. You couldn't even see the face.

'Dead?' I asked.

'Yes, Little Brother, hit and run.'

There was a smell of skokiaan oozing from the dead man. I felt like becoming sick.

'Let's go, before they blame this on us,' I urged.

'Not before you search him, Little Brother.'

'No! No!' I protested. 'It's bad luck. Besides, I'll only get my hands full of blood. It's bad luck to steal from the dead. I've never done it before.'

'You're not stealing, you're taking, Little Brother.' Everytime he referred to me as 'Little Brother', I got the impression that he was mocking me.

'Look,' I argued, 'this dead man might be our blood brother, for all we know. Why molest him?'

'Money, Little Brother, is never enough. And if the dead man is

25

our blood brother, remember, blood is only thicker than water when it runs in our veins. Once it spills, no brother wants it. So make use of the dead while you're alive. The dead die so that we may live. They have no need for money where they are going.'

Nine's philosophy. I suppose he had a point. If you read the Bible right, you'll find that Cain only started living after he had spilled Abel's blood. The only thing he hated about Abel after killing him was his blood.

'To hell with you, you heartless bastard,' I said, as I went on all fours. I searched and vomited at the same time. Then I dragged the body to the gutter, so that cars could pass.

When I stood up from my revolting task, I was shivering. There was a tobacco bag dangling from my fingers. As usual, Nine was right about it being our lucky night. The tobacco bag contained seven single pound notes and some loose change.

When we came to our room at Bertha Street, Nine counted the money on the bed. Then he went on all fours and dragged a plank suitcase from under the bed. From it he took a black money-box. The insides of the box were empty except for a tiny nickel-plated revolver.

My eyes must have bugged because he smiled crookedly.

'Like it?' he asked. I picked up the fire-arm, handling it like you would a poisonous snake.

As I examined it, Nine said, 'I prefer a knife to that. I once shot a man in the head with it at Prospect Township, and he ran all the way down the street shouting my name at the top of his voice before he dropped dead. Lucky for me nobody heard him.' He said this and dismissed it as if he'd just told me that the skokiaan we had drunk last night was too weak.

4

Sisinyana, biggest, and most respected shebeen queen of the early twenties, catered for all the subversive elements of Sophiatown. At her headquarters you found all forms of gambling from dice to the Chinese numbers game known as Fafi.

The first time that Nine took me to her place and she peeped around the door, I could only stare and stare. Man, she was beautiful! She laughed at the way I gaped. When she laughed her whole face brightened up, including the gold filling that sparkled between two sets of pearly white teeth. What laughed most was her eyes; they were baby-blue and they twinkled with all kinds of pleasant suggestions. The very sound she emitted had the tinkle of music. One look at that breathtaking face made you swear never to patronise another shebeen house.

She then opened the door wider and walked in. I very nearly screamed foul! The Maker had played a dirty trick on that woman. A deliberate blunder – a kitten with the body of a rhinoceros. I once saw her embracing and kissing a man who weighed well over a hundred and fifty till he went insane with desire, then calmly she picked him up and threw him bodily through a closed door. 'That's for taking advantage of the weaker sex,' she called after him.

Her shebeen house was about one brick cottage and two zinc shacks from where me and Nine lived. We were practically neighbours. I went there with Nine or to look for Nine. It was the only place where he hung out.

One Friday I went alone. Three quaver knocks on Sisinyana's door, and I heard a rustling sound coming from within. The door opened partly, and I saw a hole-digger concealed behind it. I pushed it open and it revealed an ill-lit passage.

I waited for the hole-digger to close the door, then followed after him down the dimly-lit passage. The passage was long and narrow. Both walls had long stripes of black soot caused by the strategically placed candles. A globeless electric cord dangled from a narrow black ceiling. In gone days, it must have been a pretty house.

On both sides of the passage, facing one another, were door frames without doors. They led to what were known as Skokiaan Drinking Rooms. These rooms were bare of furniture except for four long benches placed four-square around the room.

Whenever the police made a raid on the premises, Sisinyana would deny all ownership of them. Besides being used as skokiaan bars for skokiaan drinkers, they were also used as sleeping quarters for the cleaners, hole-diggers or barmen.

In the midst of all this squalor there was one room that was furnished like the inside of a palace, and that was Sisinyana's own room. She called it the Holy Spot because of the numerous religious pictures that were hanging from its walls. When we came to the door that led to the Holy Spot, the grave-digger, I mean hole-digger, knocked.

A voice not without melody bade us enter. As the hole-digger turned the knob, his behaviour reminded me of someone who was about to enter a sacred place. I didn't blame him, because I felt the same.

'Ah! Little Brother!' she exclaimed with genuine joy. Since my friendship with Nine, I was respected throughout Sophiatown.

'Tell me,' she said, 'is Little Brother your real name? Nine is always calling you that.'

'My name is Duggie,' I stammered. I was forever uneasy in the presence of this woman.

'Duggie?' she repeated. She rolled the name over her tongue as if fearing it would drop out of her mouth. Dreamily she said: 'Mmmmmmm Duggie, that's a nice name.'

I didn't tell her that I got the name through the circus elephant that I once looked after. The elephant's name was Duggie. Everytime the circus population called that name, me and the elephant would turn our heads in unison. That's how the name got stuck on me. My second name, which I'm using as a surname, was supplied by the Tokai reformatory authorities. They called me Kaffir Boetie. In the Africaans language it means 'little kaffir brother'. That's the name I must have given Nine the night I wanted to beat him half to death and became drunk instead.

'You know, Duggie,' said Sisinyana, 'I'm feeling low. A customer just died owing me skokiaan money. Still,' she shrugged her shoulders helplessly, 'it can't be helped, if the man had to die, he had to die. All I know is that when I die, I'll collect a fortune in hell and pay my way to heaven with it. I talk too much, I nearly forgot to give you your message from Nine. He wants you to meet him at the Johannesburg goods shed first thing in the morning, come rain or snow.'

'Isn't he here?'

She shook her lovely head. 'No! He said his loins were bothering him and the only person who can relieve him is his girl in

Moroka.' After a slight pause, she said, 'I pity the girl. Let me get you a drink.'

Moroka! Nine once took me there, and I hated the place. A city of mud and sack. It made Sophiatown look like a dream place; a difficult township to describe, or understand. A flat heap with countless alleys. Smoke from thousands of fire-galleys. The reddish-brown mud buildings looked like anything but houses. It was as if the builders had had to finish before the sun went down.

The latrines were built at a distance from the dwelling-places. As a result, when you were at a skokiaan party, and you felt the urge to relieve nature, it was best never to leave your hat behind but take it with you. The precaution was very necessary. Not because your hat was in danger of being pinched or something like that; the danger lay in the fact that you might never be able to find your way back to the same house from the latrine.

I wasn't surprised when Nine once told me that his girlfriend's neighbour used to experience considerable difficulty in finding his own house whenever he came from work. Until Nine sold him an idea. The man took a long pole and tied an old cap on the one point of the pole, then he planted the pole in front of his house. Every time he came back from work, all he did was look for the pole with the cap on.

I wasn't surprised that Nine left without me. He knew how I felt about the place.

Sisinyana, appearing with my six-inch mug of skokiaan, caught me studying a picture that was hanging over the fireplace. It was the picture of Jesus Christ on the crucifix. I thought this picture was as out of place here as it would be if it was hanging in the heart of Prince Lucifer's domain.

She looked at the picture then said: 'Oh, Him. He's Jesus Christ our Saviour, the only man I pay protection money to.'

'What kind of protection?' I asked.

Lifting her lovely eyebrows she said: 'Does it matter what kind of protection as long as I'm protected?

'You know, Duggie, I once paid protection to a white police-man and the bastard kept bleeding me even when it wasn't necessary. So I fixed him by framing him. Now he's no more bother. In fact all the police of Newlands Police Station are giving my place a wide berth.'

29

She frowned. 'Ever framed a policeman, Duggie?' When she saw me looking stupid, she said, 'Sergeant van der Merwe was the worsest among all the police of Newlands. I say was, because he's been transferred.

'One morning I was short of money to buy my stock when the bastard came in and demanded his usual cut. I tried explaining but he just wouldn't listen. Instead of understanding and coming back on Monday – because this happened on a Saturday morning – he decided to search my place. Under the mattress of my bed, he found four bottles of brandy. He wanted to take me to the charge office, but I begged off. I told him that I was still waiting for my weekly customers to come and square the books. I promised to join him later on at the charge office. He agreed because he knew I was a woman of my word. That was one time I didn't keep it. I never followed him.

'Monday morning when the court-room opened, I was there. I went in and made myself comfortable among the spectators. When the clerk of the court called my name, I stood up. The magistrate read the charge. He didn't even look up. On the desk in front of the prosecutor stood the four bottles of brandy. I hadn't even had time to doctor them. My heart went out to them. Next to them stood the cheerful van der Merwe.

'"Sisinyana," the magistrate said, "you are charged with being in possession of four bottles of brandy. How do you plead, guilty or not guilty?" He waited for the interpreter to put it across to me. Meanwhile I had heard and understood every word.

'"Four?" I said.

'"Yes, four," he said, looking directly at me. I shook my head slowly, then frowned like someone who doesn't comprehend.

'"Four," he repeated as he pointed at the four bottles of brandy on the desk. There followed a "Well?" He waited for me to say there were two or even less.

'"Your Honour," I said, "the bottles were not four, they were a dozen."

'"A what?"

'The interpreter was forgotten. It was man to man. "A dozen, Your Honour."

'"Then what the he . . . I mean, what happened to the other bottles?"

'"I don't know, Your Honour, better ask the policeman who raided my place."

'He turned to van der Merwe and asked: "Is it true what the accused claims, Sergeant – that there were twelve bottles and not four?"

'"No, Your Honour, there were only four bottles of brandy under the mattress."

'I shook my head, "Your Honour, would I want to pay for twelve bottles when I can hardly afford to pay for four? I had to search the bottom of the barrel besides running to friends and relatives for the money I have here. Money for twelve bottles."

'"How much money have you there?"

'"Knowing, Your Honour, that the fine for one bottle of brandy is fifteen pounds – and I'm going to stop selling it as I'd rather stick to skokiaan because the fine is only five pounds per four gallons – I brought along with me, Your Honour, a hundred and eighty pounds for the dozen bottles."

'The magistrate said to the prosecutor: "Count the accused's money." The prosecutor counted.

'"A hundred and eighty pounds, Your Honour."

'The magistrate then turned to Sergeant van der Merwe. "Where are the other eight bottles, Sergeant?"

'"I told Your Honour that there were only four bottles!"

'"Come now, Sergeant, are you seriously trying to tell me that this woman, or anyone for that matter, would prefer paying a fine of a hundred and eighty pounds to that of sixty? Let's not waste the court's time, where are the other eight bottles?"

'"I swear, Your Honour, there were only four bottles."

'"When you found those bottles, assuming there were four under the mattress, what did you do with them?"

'"I took them to the charge office, Your Honour."

'"Where was the accused?"

'"She was left behind, Your Honour."

'"Is that general procedure?"

'"Well, no, Your Honour, but seeing that there were only four bottles, and the accused looked to be a woman of her wor . . ."

'"Yes, yes, go on, Sergeant, you were saying?"

'"Well, Your Honour," stammered the sergeant, "she looked to be a woman of her word . . . I mean . . ."

31

'The magistrate just ignored him. "Sisinyana," he said, "I find you guilty of being in possession of four bottles of brandy. Your fine will be sixty pounds. You, Sergeant Johannes Andries van der Merwe, I find you guilty of failing to produce the other eight bottles of brandy. Corruption in the police force will never be tolerated. You will be dealt with accordingly. Next case!"

'So you see, Duggie, the only person I pay protection to is the man you see hanging there. I offer him my prayers every night before going to bed.'

I nodded, then took a deep drink from the mug of skokiaan. I gagged because of the merciless beating that my empty stomach was taking from the strong brew.

Sisinyana said: 'Easy, Duggie, don't go head-on into that stuff, try sneaking up on it.' I blinked the tears back and nodded dumbly. An old man once told me that he had once been so drunk from Sisinyana's skokiaan that he fell into a bath of cold water. The next day when he woke up, the water was lukewarm. Take it or leave it.

I fell asleep, not in a bath full of cold water, but right where I was sitting. When I woke up the following morning, it was to discover that someone had taken the trouble to cover me with a blanket. I got up, and went to the back yard in search of a water tap. I badly wanted to gargle, to stop my throat from behaving like a sewer pipe.

It was Saturday morning. The sun was shining. The air smelt clean, even in this back yard. The only sign of last night's storm lay on the ground in the form of mud, dangerous, slippery mud. Otherwise, it was a beautiful Saturday.

As I said, me and Nine were as thick as thieves, and I mean just that. When you saw Nine, you saw me. Our living came from goods trains that were parked on lonely sidings during weekdays. On Saturdays, we stripped the goods shed. The shed was big and well-provided.

Weekdays, we went to lonely sidings after dark, then I checked on the cards that were stuck on the coaches. The kind of goods that are to be found inside the coaches are tagged on the cards. The railways can be very obliging.

Mostly we found cartons of assorted cigarettes, cases containing whisky and brandy, or bales of all kinds of material. All I did was to read what was written on the cards because Nine couldn't read without glasses. Not that he ever had any.

After deciding on the required goods, Nine would swing his fifty-pound hammer, handling it as if it was a shaving machine. All he'd say to me was, 'Guard my back, Little Brother.' Then he would carry the goods to our waiting car. We hired the car from a well-known racketeer on the understanding that if we were not back by eight in the morning, he would report it stolen at the Newlands police station so that the law wouldn't confiscate the car if it was found with stolen goods. This manoeuvre wasn't bad; it saved us the trouble of really having to steal a car. The one snag about it was that if we got caught we would stand trial for two charges: theft and car theft.

We were so damned expert in this, that at times we would take orders from our Chinese customers before invading the sidings.

I made the goods shed in good time. Then I parked myself at the usual place. After waiting for a quarter of an hour, I decided to go in and see if Nine was not roaming inside. At the entrance I stopped. Something unusual was going on in the yard.

Police of both races stood in a circle excitedly discussing something that their bodies hid.

An unwanted feeling started nagging me. It touched at all my nerve centres, like the feelers of an octopus. Feelers that were getting ready for what? All I could say was that this feeling wasn't doing my kidneys any good. it kept saying, *Nine is in trouble, Nine is in trouble.*

Then I saw a lone African policeman standing at the extreme end of the yard guarding the small gate. Brushing off my trouble-some feeling, I strolled up to him. As I neared him, I made as if to pass, then suddenly I pulled up short, making as if I'd just remembered something. At the same time I noticed the round corks that were hanging from both his ears. They told me the policeman belonged to the proud Zulu race.

I greeted him in the best Zulu traditional way. According to the Zulu custom, when you want something from them, never rush them, be extremely patient and annoyingly polite.

He responded. Then I asked after his health, as if it mattered. After that, there was a long pause. I waited patiently for what seemed an age. Then the bastard took out a snuff box, tapped it

33

three times with his middle finger and said, 'To whose house do you belong?'

'I belong to Butelezi's house, Father.'

'Where?'

'At Dundee Natal, Father. We get our drinking water from the Blood River.'

'Mmmmmmm, I see, Butelezi. I'm glad to know you. I am from the house of Kuzwayo, at Eshowe Zululand. We drink from the Umvolozi River.'

'I'm happy to know you, Father.' I was lucky that he didn't give me a synopsis of the house of the Kuzwayos beginning with his great-grandfather and ending up with himself.

At last he said: 'What can I do for you, boy?' Christ! What a price to pay for a little information.

I said: 'I was just wondering at seeing so many policemen at the goods yard, Father. I'm working on the other side of the street and it's the first time for me to see so many police. Could something be wrong?'

'Yes, my son, something is very wrong here. They have at last caught the mouse that has caused the railways so much headaches. He sits in yonder circle waiting for the police van. It's a pity, my son, for the man is a warrior, a real warrior. If the two labourers and the one policeman were here, they would have agreed with me, but an ambulance carried them away. It took all those men you see standing there in a circle to subdue him, and they don't dare move away. All they did to him was daze him.' Taking a pinch of snuff, the policeman said, as if talking to himself: 'Yes, the man is a warrior.'

If the policeman had not pushed me aside, the police van would have backed into me. The van backed up until the open back door covered the little entrance neatly. They aren't taking any chances with the prisoner, I thought. I still didn't want to believe that it was Nine.

The human circle opened and a blood-covered figure was roughly pushed forward. There was no doubt about it. Blood-covered or not blood-covered, it was my Nine.

The famous grin was replaced by flaring nostrils and a heaving chest. His shackled figure was being roughly pushed from behind. When he saw me, he stopped dead. The whole dozen couldn't seem to move him. Like magic the grin came back. He lifted his manacled wrists in a farewell gesture and said: 'Look after our room, Little Brother.' With that he stepped into the van. I walked away feeling sick.

No need to tell you how I felt after the arrest of Nine. The world suddenly became a place without walls to lean on to. Like wobbling in trousers ten times too big. I had depended too much on him, now I was on my own.

5

There was a certain gang that patronised Sisinyana's shebeen. This gang always seemed to be loaded with money. They were always well-dressed and neat. Heads were shaved prison-fashion. Clean.

What I didn't like about them was that they seemed to regard going to prison as part of daily experience. A life of one year in, and the next out. They had no special speciality. They took anything that came. When they went into town, like they did every morning, they went there to take whatever the town had to offer. Handbag-snatching and pick-pocketing were their by-the-ways. Their tactics were often daring if not ruthless. One thing about them was their total indifference to consequences. Their conversation was always about their daily escapades in and around town. The first day I drank with them, I found myself listening and watching them like a dog fascinated by the activities of a bunch of snakes in a hole.

In Sophiatown we had many short cuts that could lead you from one street to the other without you having to look for a crossroad. That is, if you knew where to look for them. These short cuts were more like jigsaw puzzles because you had to go through one yard and out the other, jump a fence here and there, mind a disused skokiaan hole, and, more important, look out for human waste lest you tramp on it.

My new friends and me were using one of the short cuts. We

numbered eight in all. Among the eight, I was the only one with hair on my head. The heads of the others were all clean-shaven.

As we emerged into Gerty Street from Bertha Street, a number of African women were chatting noisily. If only one would stop and listen to what the other was saying the noise would have been much less. But they would have none of that. If one spoke the other answered or put in her own words before the other could finish. Like assorted birds in a cage. These women were runners, or agents in the Chinese game of Fafi.

They were all waiting for the Chinaman to pull the day's winning number out of his hat, then they would disperse and go and pay out or report the winning number to their clients.

This gamble has thirty-six numbers. What you have to do is guess the right number. Each number has a name. Number six, for instance, means 'Cow'. Seventeen will get you 'Diamond Lady', twenty-four, 'Big Mouth', and so on. A tickey got you six shillings, a sixpence twelve.

This is a dream game. People's dreams are responsible for the Chinaman's riches. If someone dreams he's drowning, the first thing he does in the morning is look for a Fafi agent, then place a bet on number thirteen which is 'Big Fish', he'll cover it with number three which is 'Sea Water', just in case the Chinaman draws the water instead of the fish. If you dream of silver, play 'Small Change'; a funeral means 'Dead Man'. It's a hell of a racket. All the Chinaman hopes for is that we go on having sweet dreams.

How's this for a story that went around the townships? A woman once dreamed a strange dream. The day following, she scraped every penny in the house to play a certainty. The money amounted to ten pounds, rent money and all. This she took and placed on one number. When her husband came home from work, she told him about her strange dream and what she had done with the money. The man was dog-tired from work, but he felt he wasn't too tired to strangle her. He did. He killed her. The irony of the thing is, as her breath left her body, a car door banged outside and a voice came through the open window from the street saying: 'Hey, Bengu! Your wife broke my bank – she won!'

Anyway, we ducked into the next yard, nearly upsetting a

36

fire-galley. Through an open window came the strains of blues music played on a gramophone, while behind a tall zinc fence someone was banging and yelling for another shilling's worth of skokiaan.

One by one we squeezed ourselves between the walls of two houses. We had to move sideways. As I brushed the dust from my front and back, dust caused by the tight squeeze of two walls, the din around me told me that we were in Good Street.

It was as busy as ever. Buses were lined from one corner of the street to the other. They came in different shades; red, green and blue. These buses belong to different companies. As a result, loading competition was fierce. A conductor would try to force a passenger into his bus, while the other conductor would work just as hard at dragging the individual into *his* bus. A voice would shout above the other, 'Don't go into that bus, can't you see it'll never reach town?' The other would come back with: 'Your mother will never reach town, you get in here!'

Then the hair-raising journey to town would follow, one bus trying to get there first, so as to be first to load again.

We entered a Syrian café. I was surprised to see Jeegar, the undisputed leader of our gang, cutting right through the shop and going through a back door as if he owned the place. We followed him through. I found myself in a room with a long table and two benches.

Jeegar ordered breakfast. Fried steak and eggs. Not knowing how to handle a fork and a knife, I asked for a spoon. I don't remember ever having had such tasty food in my life. I made a mental note to frequent this place whenever I found myself in the money. This was no thick-porridge-and-meat café, this was a place for the real upper class.

After breakfast, we crossed the street and caught the first bus into town.

In town, we got off at the Diagonal Street bus terminal. On that same side of the bus terminal were rows of shops, mostly barber shops. We entered one of them. It was owned by a Rhodesian who went under the name of Black Mischark because of his blue-black complexion.

Before having my head shaved so as to be in uniform with the rest of the gang, I was introduced to Black Mischark. He didn't

37

wear a shirt. His protruding stomach was covered by a soiled undershirt. Mischark, I was told, harboured whatever goods we brought in from town.

While Mischark was shaving my head, the boys entered some cubicles that stood like telephone booths in the shop. When they emerged, they were dressed in khaki dustcoats. The dustcoats had red letters printed on the shoulder blades such as K & B, S & C, and so on. By all appearances they looked like city workers. My admiration for them increased.

Jeegar and Madaku were going to take the top part of town. Twala and Mabongo would concentrate on the centre, while me and Tiny looked after the bottom half, near the post office and also part of Johannesburg Station. T-Boy and Thabo had the Indian market. A dangerous place because it's always crowded. Only the night before I heard Jeegar say, 'When you are being chased at the Indian market, never forget to run with your knife open.'

Me and Tiny crossed Frazer Street, heading towards the other side of town. We were going to start at the top, then work our way back towards the bus-rank. At the corner of Bree and Loveday Streets, I saw a group of people, white and black, standing in a semicircle looking at one black man who sat with his back against the wall. Closer inspection showed the man sitting on his haunches fanning three playing-cards at his audience, daring them to find the red card amongst the two blacks.

This form of gambling is known as the Red Find. The gambler throws three cards face-down on the ground; all you have to do is place a pound note, or even less, on the card you think is red. If it is, you win an extra pound.

'Duggie, watch.' It was Tiny. He elbowed his way to the front. I followed. From his pocket he extracted a tiny roll of pounds. Publicly he selected one, making sure that the gambler saw the roll.

The man picked up the cards. With one twist of the wrist the cards lay face down. I noted the red card, so did Tiny. In fact, so did most of the crowd, because they all pointed excitedly. Tiny was about to place his bet when a man standing next to him blocked him with his foot at the same time saying: 'I saw it first.' He placed three pounds on the card. The gambler opened the card;

it was red. The crowd applauded. The lucky man won three pounds. I think I saw Tiny grin, but I'm not sure.

Down came the cards again, I thought the man next to Tiny was going to block him again, but he didn't. Nor did Tiny place a bet. A black, fat, grinning woman came forward and placed a pound on a card. When the gambler turned it up, the card was black. There were cries of 'Shame' from the crowd.

Down went the cards again. I noticed Tiny watching the foot of the man more than he did the cards. As soon as the cards were settled face-down, the man tried lifting his foot, but Tiny's right foot was resting firmly on it.

Tiny placed five dirty-looking single pound notes on a card. The gambler swallowed hard as he looked up. He was sweating. I could see the white behind his eyeballs.

'Open up!' shouted the crowd gleefully. 'Open up!' He did. The card was red.

Tiny lifted his foot. I saw the gambler looking daggers at the man next to Tiny.

After counting and pocketing the winnings, Tiny said, 'The bloody Shangaan bastard – he only came to Joburg yesterday and he thinks he can con me!'

'Why didn't you stay to press your luck, Tiny?'

'Luck?' scoffed Tiny. 'That would have been inviting trouble. There's no such a thing as luck in that game, Duggie. You get back there you'll see so many black cards that you'll really see red – and I don't mean the red card, I mean the man's blood. Putting your money on the red card is like supporting a child that's not your own.

'You saw the man that was standing next to me?' When I nodded, Tiny went on: 'That man is a decoy. There are two others and a girl. If you spot the right card, either the girl or that man will block you. Place your bet on the wrong card, and they won't interfere with you. That's a no chance game, Duggie, that's a sure game. Because the right card is like looking for a needle in the wrong haystack.'

Tiny changed the subject by saying, 'Duggie, have you ever picked pockets before?'

'I've tried my hand.' I shuddered, remembering Honest Charley's meat cleaver.

'O.K., let me tell you how we go about it. The trouble is, we are only two instead of three. It's all right if we are going to do ordinary pickpocketing, but when we go "square" hunting, we need three. The square is the small purse inside the big one. When we are three it's one of the easiest things to take. Even if the bag is clipped. But when we are only two it's a bit risky.

'First, never try lifting a square on the pavement. Always check on the robots before you make your move. If the robot shows red, we close in on the woman. One of us will be on each side of her on the kerb. The "square" man will be slightly behind her. The "jolter" – I mean the man who distracts her attention by elbowing her in the ribs – will be on her left side. The "pincer" – he's the one who opens the bag – will be on her right. Coming from the opposite direction towards us will be the "square-puller". When the light shows green we move. Never take the victim until you are in the middle of the street. You see, her nervousness about motor cars helps.

'The jolter will jolt, she'll look up only to be met by a "Sorry, madam". This gives the "can-opener" a chance to unbuckle the bag. At the same time the square-puller will come in between them and lift the square. We never miss, because there's no stopping, no hesitating, no pausing, it's just one smooth movement. Clear, straight and neat.'

I was still mulling over what Tiny had told me when we arrived at Von Brandis Street on the side of the General Post Office.

Suddenly Tiny stopped dead. I followed his gaze and was in time to see a white man emerging from the post office entrance. The man was busy stuffing a fat-looking wallet into his jacket inside pocket. Tiny looked around wildly, then said as he dashed into the post office yard, 'Don't let him out of your sight!'

When Tiny came back, he was breathless. In his hands he held a cardboard box. This he trampled flat by stamping on it with both feet. He gave me the feeling that he was losing his reason, but it couldn't be, because he had been talking sense only a few minutes before.

'Here,' he said, shoving the now flat board towards me. 'Take this and hit me on the head with it. Hit hard, don't be afraid that it'll hurt – it won't. It's only cardboard. Now go on and hit me.' I hesitated. It's hard to play at being mad when you know damn well that you're sane.

'Go on, damn you, you're wasting time!' he shouted. Half-heartedly I lifted the cardboard.

Wham! The blow was clumsy. Tiny ran. Wham! Wham! He screamed. Not knowing why, I started beating him earnestly. He zig-zagged towards the white man who had emerged from the post office and was now walking towards Small Street. Tiny was drawing a lot of attention to himself by screaming 'Hey! Heh!' at the top of his voice. Wham! Wham! Everybody turned and looked as I rained murderous blows on Tiny's clean-shaven head. I managed to get in two more blows just as Tiny reached the white man.

I was beginning to enjoy myself, even though I didn't know where all this was leading to. Wham! went the cardboard. Wham! Wham! Wham! almost with rhythmical precision.

'Please help me, my baas,' sobbed Tiny. 'He's hurting me!' Wham! There was real fear in Tiny's eyes as I continued my assault.

The khaki dustcoat, with the letters S & H printed on the shoulder blades and the red dust rag sticking out of one of his pockets, gave Tiny the appearance of a hard-working African, while I had the look of a loafer. There was also the determined look in my eyes, as I hailed blow after blow on Tiny's unprotected head.

Tiny held the strange white man from behind. He was vainly trying to use him as a shield. He was handling the man just as you would handle the steering wheel of a get-away car in heavy traffic.

Wham! went the cardboard as it glanced off the shoulder of the bewildered white man. Face reddening with embarrassment, the white man said, 'Hey! Boy! Leave this boy alone!' He was helplessly trying to look at Tiny over his shoulders. He said to Tiny, 'You, too, leave me alone!'

Wham! Another bull's-eye. It landed squarely on Tiny's head. Wham! Wham! Wham! Tiny couldn't take any more. 'Yooooh!' he screamed as he let go of his only protection and ran down Jeppe Street. Behind, the white man sighed with relief as he straightened out his jacket lapels. Then slowly his mouth opened as if his lips were gummed together.

41

'My wallet! My wallet!' he screamed. Wham! Wham! echoed the cardboard box as we raced across Von Brandis Street, completely disregarding the red light, in the direction of the Indian market and the Sophiatown bus-rank.

This market is one place where I like to be. I could wander about it the whole day and never get tired or bored with it. Here there's never a dull moment. The fruit stalls with their crafty-looking owners, their high-pitched voices forever urging passers-by to examine and buy their fruit. This place is a symbol of life, guile and greed.

Later, as we walked along Diagonal Street looking for something to eat, Tiny nudged me. He pointed to a small car that was parked next to the pavement.

A European woman was sitting in the driver's seat behind the steering-wheel. Lying negligently next to her was her handbag. That was not the real attraction, the real attraction was the window beside the bag. It was open.

Sitting in the back seat and looking lost, was her African servant. I made a bee-line for the opened window, while Tiny walked directly towards the woman. 'Lies, lies, that's all you told me! I told you one day we'll meet and I'll mess you up! When you are at the missus' yard you tell a lot of lies. You got a lot to say, all lies! Come out of there!'

'What's the matter? What has he done to you? Leave my boy alone!'

Ignoring her, Tiny continued threatening the boy, who, because of fright, started working his jaws and saying nothing.

'What has he done to you?' asked the madam indignantly.

'I'm not talking to you, missus.'

'But I'm talking to you! What has my boy done to you?'

'I told him one day he'll get hurt.' Tiny made as if to open the door.

'You leave my car alone . . .' I lifted the bag.

As we walked back to the bus-rank my hunger was completely forgotten. Tiny said, 'Serves her right for not allowing him to sit next to her.'

6

At Sisinyana's place the skokiaan bubbles were floating pleasantly up and down my stomach. Every time I belched, one would pop, spreading heavenliness throughout my body.

I was in high spirits. The white man's wallet had yielded forty pounds and the woman's bag, twelve.

When Jeegar came in, heavily laden with two suitcases, my happiness knew no bounds. The straps around the cases told me that they belonged to a commercial traveller. Jeegar was followed by Marfaku, who was likewise burdened.

I asked a foolish question, because I was very excited. 'What's in there?'

'How the hell should I know?' growled Jeegar, at the same time giving me a dirty look. I didn't care, I was far too happy to feel offended.

I never liked Jeegar. When we first met, it was hate at first sight. He was a brutal bastard. I once saw him stab a girl for spilling some skokiaan on him.

I helped to open the suitcases. Jeegar groaned. First I didn't understand his dismay. The suitcases were full of gent's shoes. All different designs. Then I added my groan to Jeegar's. The shoes all belonged to the same foot, the right. The second suitcase had ladies' one-sided shoes, the suitcases that Marfaku had were crammed with boys' and girls' one-sided shoes. Jeegar cursed. 'Bloody samples!' he growled.

From that day onward, I never had a dull moment. Tiny was the perfect partner. We were a faultless team. It was as if I was born for nothing but this kind of work.

We ravaged the town. Our success lay mainly in what the brain doctors call telepathy. We never asked questions or discussed a situation while on the job. One always seemed to know what the other was thinking. Our timing was perfect. We didn't plan in

43

advance. We thought on the spot. The word hesitation was considered a deadly enemy.

Jeegar was a good pickpocket, but Tiny was the best. If Jeegar picked a pocket and the victim found out, he beat hell out of the victim. Not Tiny. Tiny went about it with an elastic sense of humour.

He once pinched a purse and, finding it empty, walked up to the victim and said: 'Lady, here's your purse. Next time don't decorate the inside of your bag with an empty purse – keep something in it. Think of all the risks I have to take.'

He surprised me once as we were walking down Plein Street. I wasn't even aware that he had made a pinch when he suddenly stopped short like someone who had forgotten or just remembered something.

'Wait!' he said. He ran back in the direction we had come from. After a few minutes he was back.

'What's up?' I asked.

Grinning, he said, 'I forgot to close her bag.'

Me, I still have to discover my true talent. Because I discovered painfully that picking pockets is not one of them.

This happened at von Weilligh Street. I was about to cross it when I saw an elderly Jewish woman also about to cross. I knew by her hawk-like features that she was Jewish, and where else do you find the biggest egg if not in a hawk's nest?

After nudging Tiny, I went for her. I was going to take her in the middle of the street like I was taught. Tiny veered off to the left to divert while I took her.

All went well, but I bungled by being too damn curious. I couldn't control my patience, I wanted to see how much money was in the damn purse. I was itching all over. My breath was hot with excitement. So right there where I took it I stopped and peeped inside while cars hooted. I was pocketing it when I felt a heavy hand gripping my shoulder.

I didn't turn. I just took a quick look at what was pressing so painfully into my collar bone. I saw hairy fingers as big as corn cobs. What was frightening was the colour of the fingers. They were pinkish white.

My first guess was right. The hand belonged to a white man. I dislike guessing, because I usually guess right when I'm doing

44

wrong, and wrong when I'm doing right. What caused me to look up behind me for the second time was the silver star I saw on the helmet. It held my gaze more than the hostile blue eyes that were boring into me.

Miserably I guessed again. My second guess was that this was a policeman. Another bull's-eye. If only I could guess like that when I played the Chinese numbers game then there would be no point in me picking pockets.

'Madam!' shouted the policeman after the woman. 'Is this your purse?' He lifted my hand still holding the purse high above my head. I felt the tips of my toes helplessly scraping the tarmac. I wondered whether he was more interested in severing my arm from my body, or in giving the purse back to the owner. I concluded he was interested in both.

Much against my will another unpleasant guess escaped. This guess caused me to moan. I guessed that his hand was bigger than a cow's bladder. I was right. Police all over the world are chosen mainly for their size, not for their brains. God doesn't give a man brains as well as size; I have never known Him to be so generous.

'Madam! Your purse!'

I hereby swear to do my duty, to my God, my King and my country, the son of a bitch, I thought.

'Madam, your purse!' I couldn't even struggle in this man's hold.

The woman looked around, then cursed in a strange language. Frantically she started rummaging in her bag, rummaging and talking at the same time. The only sensible word that invaded her strange dialect now and again was the word 'Officer'.

It's funny, when you're frightened or angry beyond control you learn a lot about your origins. That's how I discovered to what black race I belong; something I never used to take notice of before. When I use strong language, Xhosa comes easier, so maybe originally my ancestors were Xhosas. Not that I care a damn. I remember when I first saw myself in a long mirror at a chemist shop. I was passing and suddenly there I was; ragged and dirty, yet getting a kick at what I saw. In Sophiatown all the boys of my age looked like that. Rags were our uniform. With a smile and giggle I hopped away from the mirror.

Looking up from her fruitless search, the white woman snatched the purse from my grasp then opened it with fingers that shook uncontrollably. All this told me that I had just lost a fortune because of a good Dutch Samaritan bastard.

Looking up from counting the money, she said, 'Thank you, Officer; the money, it is all here.' Next, she turned and elbowed her way through the curious onlookers.

'Hey! Wait!' yelled the policeman, still holding on to me. 'You've got to come to the Marshall Square police station to lay a formal charge against this kaffir.'

'Sorry, Officer,' came from the woman. 'I'm in a hurry; besides, I'm not missing a penny.' With that, she turned and disappeared through the crowd.

The crowd, most of it black, started laughing and jeering at the policeman. I didn't like that, especially when I saw what anger was doing to his complexion; it was beet-red.

Then lightning struck in the form of a fist. It landed on the side of my head. I wanted to drop and cover my face, but couldn't. How could I when I was dangling six inches from the ground, a rag doll in the man's hands? He chopped me on the bridge of the nose with the cutting side of his hand. The stars I saw were unlike the one on his helmet; they were tiny and numerous and they glittered in a sort of liquid transparent blue. What was maddening about them was that they couldn't seem to keep still, when one popped another moved in. Then through a bemused brain I heard a voice say, '*Gee him vir my konstabel* – give him to me!'

A right that must have broken my jaw sent me flying into the hands of another obliging son of a bitch. I was not unconscious. I should have been, but I was not. Because dimly I could hear a crowd of people shouting, 'Lock him up! Don't beat him up, lock him up, you bloody cowards!' I didn't agree; being locked up in jail after what I was going through was unfair.

I found myself lying under a car. I must have crawled in there for sanctuary from the cruelty of the world in general. Tiny's voice came faintly to my ears as if from another world.

'Come out, Duggie, they're gone. God knows they're gone! Come out, man!'

'Bugger you, leave me alone!' Opening my mouth nearly caused me to pass out.

'Look, Duggie,' he said. 'Here's my cross.' He had gone down

46

on all fours. Awkwardly he pushed his crossed fingers under the car for me to see.

The sign of the cross to us blacks in South Africa is a sacred symbol. The dirtiest liar uses crossed fingers to show sincerity by crossing both his first fingers from the thumb. A sign that he means what he says. After moving my jaws sideways twice, I decided to ignore Tiny's crossed fingers and to stay right where I was. A crossed jaw is more painful than crossed fingers. It was only when he said that the owner of the car was coming to move his car that I saw the sense of crawling from my sanctuary.

Instead of leading me home or to the hospital, Tiny led me to a place known as Malay Camp. This area rubbed elbows with Johannesburg City. It was a semi-slum, and metropolitan in a way like Sophiatown. Where Sophiatown had shanties and mud buildings, Malay Camp boasted wooden double-storey buildings. Here you could buy a woman of any colour. It was your money that counted. Take away the tar roads and the electricity and you had one of those American Wild West towns that we see so much of in the bioscope. Only here, wine bottles flew, not bullets.

Tiny insisted that all I needed was a drink. If I could have moved my jaws I would have argued, but you can't argue with a broken jaw. The pain made me walk like a man in a trance. Talking was out of the question, hearing was annoying; feeling only meant additional blinding pain, and thinking was outright misery. Shit, I was sure I was dying.

Before we could reach a shebeen, Tiny became conscious of the seriousness of my condition. If passersby hadn't stopped to stare at me, it's doubtful if he would have done what he did. He hired a taxi, bundled me in and rode with me to the General Hospital. I was fitted with wires around my jaws to keep them in place.

After spending three weeks at home drinking soup through a straw, I went back to the hospital where they removed the wiring.

This part which I am about to relate is the only part of my life which I can't seem to believe myself, because history doesn't repeat itself so soon; at least, not just after three weeks of broken

47

jaws. But if the truth has to come out, then I have no alternative but to set down on paper all the events that took place, even if there might be a ring of fantasy in them.

'How do you like the town, Duggie, after three whole weeks at home?'

'I don't.'

It was Tiny talking, we were walking down Bree Street in the direction of Doornfontein. There was a bitter feeling in me. I don't know whether it was caused by failure to prove myself, or just plain fear.

Tiny was penniless. I had a shilling piece somewhere in one of my pockets.

He interrupted my troubled thoughts by saying, 'Give me one of your cigarettes, Duggie.'

Shaking my head, I said, 'I wish I had some, Tiny.'

The tips of my fingers went into the top small pocket of my jacket where I kept stubs. They came out empty. I went through all my pockets with the same results. Then my fingers met with the shilling piece.

I looked around and spied a tea room. I went inside.

In the shop, lined next to the counter, stood five Africans, all dressed in blue overalls. In their hands were empty jam tins for tea-buying purposes. Daily customers, I thought. Just behind sat European customers having their lunch.

I took a place next to the first African. I didn't want to waste time. I rapped the shilling piece on the glass counter to draw the owner's attention. If you irritate them that way, they quickly get rid of you by serving you first.

'Packet of ten Lotus, please.' He gave me the packet. I handed over the shilling. He was about to give me my four pennies change and there the matter would have ended. But fate took a hand. Just before he gave me my change, he was urgently beckoned by one of his servants. Instead of giving me my change he answered the summons.

Then I saw it. I didn't see it before because his body had been screening it. A roll of pounds as thick as my wrist lay just within arm's reach. It was tied with a rubber band.

I must have been a born thief. A real stranger to hesitation, with impulses that work overtime. Without thinking or looking

48

around, my hand shot out like the tongue of a deadly cobra. At the same time I sensed rather than saw Tiny inspecting the window display just outside the shop entrance.

It was fast. Too damn fast, especially for the naked eye. One minute the roll was in my hand, the next it was sailing through the air towards Tiny, who caught it expertly and without thinking. Then he slowly made his way to the opposite pavement.

I was about to bolt through the door after Tiny, but when I looked at the African next to me, I saw to my amazement that he wasn't a bit concerned with me. Instead, he was grumbling to his fellow worker about the slowness of the Greek. It was unbelievable, yet it happened. NO ONE SAW ME!

I decided to wait for my change.

When the Greek came back, the first thing he noticed was that the money was missing. Next, he looked at me. The look he gave me made me curse myself for still being where I was. What kept me rooted to the spot still disturbs me right up to this day.

Without a word he went around the counter and bolted the door, surprising everyone in the café. Then he told the Africans to point out the one who took the money. They all denied having seen the money, let alone having stolen it.

After careful searching each of them, he told them to go. Then he turned to me. Before touching me he told me to give back the money. I told him I didn't have any money. As always when I'm truthful he just didn't believe me.

'Look,' he said as he released a long-held breath. His body bent sideways and he leaned with his elbow on the glass counter. 'I know you have the money even if I didn't see you take it. Now let's be sensible; if you give me the money of your own free will, I promise to let you go and there the matter will end. But if I search you and find it on you, I'll make you suffer.'

'Go to hell! I haven't got your money, but you got mine, you got my fourpenny change.'

'Listen, for the last time, give me the money.' I stood my ground.

Then he searched me. He didn't find anything, of course. How could he when the money was on the other side of the street?

'Now give me my change,' I said, full of confidence.

'You stay right there,' he said.

He was picking on me because those other Africans were his daily customers, also, I was nicely dressed, in a way. My clothes alone made me suspect number one, also the fact that it was my first time in his bloody shop. He was bright, but in a dull way.

Again he searched me. This time he was more careful. When he didn't find anything, he went to the phone and rang for the police. While we waited, he kept on pestering me about his money, promising to let me go if I showed him where it was.

I told him I didn't know anything about any money. That the only money I knew of was my four pennies change. And that still had to come to me.

I was more sure of myself. My only prayer was that they wouldn't send the same policeman who broke my jaw the month before. The Greek could go to hell. He wasn't going to get any money from me even if he borrowed it.

There was a sharp rap on the door and in they came. I mean the police. It wasn't the same one as before. This one was even bigger. With him was another one with a young pink face.

'Where is the kaffir?' he asked. The Greek indicated with his head towards where I stood.

He turned to me and bellowed, 'Where is the money, kaffir?' I told him too that I didn't know anything about any money except for four pennies change. The child policeman came nearer me and started jabbing me in the ribs with his baton. I kept facing the burly one who kept repeating the question. I was about to repeat that I didn't know anything about any money when they started working on me.

Suddenly, I heard a female voice scream, 'Stop! Stop! Can't you see you're killing him?'

The burly policeman said, 'Keep out of this lady, it's none of your business.'

'Where's the money, kaffir?'

'No money, baas, only my change.'

'You'll talk, you black bastard.'

My face was so numb, it didn't seem to hurt anymore. It lost all sense of feeling.

He was throttling me with the front of my shirt by screwing it into my Adam's apple.

I heard the lovely voice again, now more furious, 'Of course it's my business. I was sitting right here when this whole filthy business started!'

'Lady, for God's sake,' said the policeman impatiently. 'Will you for God's sake keep out of this?'

Squinting, I saw a white woman glaring at my tormentors with bared teeth, hair drooping over eyelids and arms resting palm-down on the table. She was spitting out words faster than a green snake could spit poison. And the words were just as venomous. The way she went on, it was as if she was suffering more than I was. A lovely bundle of fury.

'The fact that I was sitting right here when this whole thing started makes it my business.'

'Lady, for the last time, mind your own business.' I began to wonder if those were the only words he knew.

'To begin with, that boy didn't take the blasted money.'

'How do you know?' scowled the policeman.

'Because it's a logical if not a physical impossibility for him to have taken the money.'

'Lady, you're not telling me anything.'

'If,' continued my guardian angel, 'God did not use some of your brains to give you a bigger backside, you would have arrived at the same conclusion. Stop behaving like a third-rate bully and start using your head!'

'Madam, one more word out of you and I'll run you in for obstructing the police in the course of their duty.'

'Since when does duty mean beating up a man who hasn't been formally charged, and on private premises for that matter? In fact you are so brainless that I believe you would make a fool of yourself in front of your superiors by locking me up for trying to help you!'

As the man straightened up, I saw that his trouser at the knee was wet with my blood.

'All right, lady,' he said harshly. 'You tell us what happened to the money.'

'I can give you a hundred reasons why it is absurd to think that this poor boy could have taken the money. But three should be enough for a brain like yours!'

Then she went into detail. It was like a school teacher explaining a simple subject to a sixteen-year-old pupil who had no business in the third grade.

'That boy was searched twice yet the money was not found. If, as you say, he took the money, then where in heaven's name could he have hidden it? Because,' said my lady with great emphasis and spacing every word, 'he never once left the shop, nor did he move from where you found him! Tell me, now,' she was almost begging, 'do you for one minute think that if anyone could steal a roll of pounds he'd be so stupid as to stand and wait for a measly fourpence change when the door was wide open and he had every chance of running away? I,' she spat, 'would give everything I possess – and I can assure you it's considerable –' (Chancer, I thought) 'if that boy is guilty of theft.' I stole a glance at the other customers and saw most of them nodding their heads in agreement.

The burly policeman said, 'Then who the hell has stolen the money?'

'That's the first sensible question you've asked since coming through that door! Now kindly direct that same question to the man who phoned for you. For all we know, he might not have lost a penny, it's just his word against this poor boy's.'

The law turned his eyes from the lady to the Greek and there was fury in them.

The shopkeeper said to the lady, 'Do you think I would have gone to all the trouble of searching the natives and calling the police all for nothing?'

'There! You have done it!' said my lady triumphantly.

'Did you really lose money?' asked the policeman facing the shopkeeper.

'Of course!' spluttered the man indignantly.

'Show me the spot where the money was.' The man pointed at the spot behind the counter. The policeman released his hold on me for the first time, leaving me to sway with the tide. Examining the spot, the policeman asked, 'Was he the only kaffir that was standing next to the counter at the time?' Worriedly the shop-keeper shook his head.

'There were four or five others,' he added hastily, 'but those were my daily customers. They would not steal from me.'

'What!' barked the policeman, throwing his hands in the air in a hopeless show of disgust. 'Are you standing there telling me that kaffirs don't steal when they were born for nothing else? Why did you let the rest of them go?'

There was a note of anger in the shopkeeper's voice as he said, 'I tell you those other natives are my daily customers, and this boy, well, you can see for yourself how he's dressed, he's a skellum.'

'Now you're judging the man by his clothes!' came the voice of my guardian angel.

'If I remember right, those boys that were here were in a much better position to have made off with the money! They were all dressed in overalls – right! And in their hands they carried jam tins – right! Jam tins full of tea bought from this shop! It's my guess that the roll of pounds – if he did lose a roll of pounds – is safely reposing at the bottom of a jam tin of tea!'

The big policeman started to say something, when an eager voice from the cradle said, 'Should I lock up this kaffir?'

'No, better let him go. What will we charge him with? We've already messed up his face.'

Turning to me, the policeman said, 'Scoot, kaffir.' I slowly shook my head and stood my ground. Glaring at me he said, 'Well, what the hell are you waiting for?'

Through bloody, swollen lips I said, 'My fourpenny change.'

Turning to the Greek he asked, 'Has he got change coming?'

'Yes, he gave me a shilling for an eightpenny packet of cigarettes.'

From his pocket he selected four pennies and threw them at me. I picked up the pennies and counted them carefully before pocketing them.

7

If my brains were not as dry as the marrow in a witch doctor's fortune-telling bones, I would have gone and joined the queue at the Labour Exchange Department with a view to getting myself some honest employment, instead of listening to what Tiny was saying. Something told me that one day Tiny was going to get me into a lot of trouble.

I was two days out of hospital, after three months there. What kept disturbing me was what the doctor said just as I was preparing to leave. His actual words were, 'From now on, and for a good long time to come, know that there is very little difference between your jaw and a piece of cut glass, because that's what your jaw has become, and that's what it's going to be for a very long time.'

Tiny was saying, 'What you need, Duggie, is a . . .'

'Good steady job,' I interrupted.

'No! No! Man, I didn't mean that.'

'Well, I meant it,' I said, giving him a mean look.

'You want to go and work for twelve shillings and sixpence a week, Duggie?'

'Yes!'

Ignoring my answer he said, 'What I was going to say is that what you need is a good witch doctor with a strong medicine. You see the monkey's skin that's tied around Jeegar's right wrist? He got that from his witch doctor; it's powerful stuff. It brings him luck.'

'Is that why he stole two suitcases full of one-sided shoes?' I asked.

'Aw, Duggie, don't talk shit, man. You're bitter, that's all.' Brightening up, he said, 'Look, I got one, too. Only mine hangs around my neck.'

'If I'm going to hang anything around my neck, Tiny, it's going to be a rosary, and not a piece of juju that's going to explode in my face.'

'You can't hang the work of Christ around your neck and expect him to help you in devil's work, Duggie. Stealing is devil's work. You got to have him around your neck if you want him to protect you.'

'What I intend doing, Tiny, won't need the Devil's protection or a monkey's skin around my wrist.'

Stupidly he asked, 'What are you going to do, Duggie?'

'Work my fingers to the bone.'

'Look, Duggie, just give me one chance to prove to you that this stuff works. Tomorrow we'll go to my witch doctor and I'll ask him to prepare one for you. After that, you'll see, nothing will ever happen to you.'

Nothing did happen to me, that is, if nothing means going in and out of prisons as if prisons had back doors.

Me and Tiny started again. That is, after I had made it clear to him that I didn't want to have anything to do with picking pockets. Lucky charm or no lucky charm, I was going to go through life openly, no sneak-thief stuff. Not even elbowing the victim so that Tiny could go to work. My cut-glass jaw came before a dirty little bag around my neck.

'Johannes,' said the white man loudly as he got out of his car at the noisy Indian market. He was talking to his African servant who was sitting next to him in the front seat because the back seat was crammed with suitcases. 'Look after the things in the car while I go into this building.'

'Yes, baas,' said Johannes.

Tiny heard the white man. So did I. Dressed in his khaki dustcoat, Tiny followed the white man into the building.

A second later, Tiny appeared. He shouted, 'Johannes, your baas wants you! Come, hurry!' Without waiting to see what Johannes' reaction would be, Tiny turned and walked back towards the building's entrance. Johannes, fearing that he might lose Tiny in the crowd, followed. He didn't suspect a thing. If his baas didn't send Tiny, then where the hell did Tiny get his name from?

Johannes was just about to enter the building when I sprang into action. I emptied the back seat of all the suitcases at the same time, praying that they did not contain one-sided shoes. I was putting the last one on the pavement when Tiny joined me.

As we were carrying the suitcases towards Black Mischark's barber shop, I said, 'What happened to Johannes?'

'I took him into the building, there was an elevator but it was written "Europeans Only", so I showed him the stairs. I left him climbing to the fourth floor.'

The white man of South Africa suffers from a defect which can be easily termed limited intelligence. The cause of this mental handicap can be safely attributed to a frustrated background of poor beginnings.

I say this because no man, no matter how dense, will allow

himself to be taken in twice by the same trick. They don't learn by mistakes, for the simple reason that they'd rather die than talk about their mistakes. Me, I learn by my mistakes because human beings make mistakes, and I'm a human being. Their pride is based on colour, and it's on this pride that we blacks feed ourselves. Call him 'Baas' and he'll break an arm to help you.

He takes advantage of his white skin, we take advantage of his crownless kingdom.

'Baas, can you please tell me where this address is?' That would be Tiny, showing a crudely-written address under the nose of a railway truck driver, while we hovered at the back like a pack of hungry wolves waiting for the kill.

It was either difficult, painful, or degrading to have to admit to a black man that he couldn't read. Whatever it was, I'll never know. What I do know is that he'd turn that envelope round and round, and make senseless sounds through his blocked nostrils, while we unloaded the trailer at the back.

Finally he'd say to Tiny, giving back the envelope. 'Tell your baas to write better or go back to school.' If Tiny didn't hear the all-clear signal from us, he'd go on making conversation with the driver.

'Doesn't this look like an "E," baas?'

The driver would take the envelope back from Tiny to have another look, then he would give it back to Tiny with a 'Yes,' adding with some finality, 'Now go back to your baas and tell him to write better.'

'But . . .'

'Go! Can't you see I'm busy?'

The all-clear whistle would come floating to Tiny's ear. Tiny would shrug his shoulders muttering, '*Dankie*, baas.'

The driver speaking to himself would say, 'Poor kaffirs, wonder what they'll do without us.' Sometimes I wonder, too.

Knowing the white man, we never bothered to change our method. They were not going to talk, and we were not going to change.

We were hitting the railways so mercilessly that they decided to hire a second white man. One that sat on top of the goods at the back of the trailer.

Another mistake. They should have given the look-out jobs to black men, men who have long discovered that only sticks and stones break bones, not abusive words. When we saw our first trailer with a guard behind, we couldn't help laughing. The guard scowled. The scowl gave Tiny an idea.

Tiny's body was small, I doubt if he weighed more than a hundred and ten. That must be the reason why he was named Tiny. I could give him a hiding with both my hands tied.

What Tiny did was to go up to the guard and volubly describe his mother's anatomy. The guard would go beet-red. He'd jump off the trailer and chase Tiny down the street with murderous intent while we off-loaded.

We did this every day, though sometimes the results were not a hundred per cent successful. Tiny would meet a watchman whose abusive language was equally good. So, instead of giving chase, he would fling the words right back.

Then Jeegar started something. Something so good, that it never failed. All Tiny had to do was to go up to the guard and spit in his face. Christ! Then he ran. Not just for the sake of running, but for his very life.

After disposing of the goods at Black Mischark's place, we used to go to Babes's car park for a drink of good pure brandy. Sisinyana's brandy was becoming more poisonous as she became richer. She had long stopped using cigarettes for mixing purposes. She was using pipe tobacco instead. She claimed that cigarettes were too expensive.

Babes worked as a car attendant at a parking lot. He collected parking fees. As a sideline he sold back-door brandy for Shamba. 'Back-door' meant something you took out through the back door where you worked. Shamba worked at a liquor store just opposite Babes's car park.

Unlike Sisinyana's, Shamba's brandy was pure, because there was very little time to doctor it. Besides, it came from directly opposite.

When we got to Babes's car park, he took us to a beautiful black sedan chair. The owner must have been very rich. Babes opened the back door, and me and Tiny climbed in.

From the cubby-hole of the expensive car came a sealed half-bottle of brandy, and from the pockets of his white dustcoat he produced a tin mug. He left us to go and guide a small car in. While we were drinking, we heard Babes scolding a female driver.

'Madam!' came his voice. 'Can't you see you're reversing into someone's car? You'll damage that head-lamp. What do you use for a driving licence – the rent receipt of your flat, or did you buy a licence?'

Just then I saw Shamba's dwarf-like body dodging between cars, and making for ours. His head appeared at our car window. He was a tiny, grinning man with a crinkly goatee, dressed in oversized overalls. He looked like a circus clown.

He opened the back door of the sedan and seated himself next to Tiny, grinning from ear to ear. His goatee was bobbing up and down.

'Where's Babes?' he asked breathlessly.

'Scolding a white lady,' grinned Tiny.

'Look, Tiny, help me with this bottle of brandy, it's hanging between my shoulder blades. Quick! Before the baas misses me.'

After Tiny got the bottle out, Shamba opened the door and scrambled out. Before re-closing the door, he said, 'Give it to Babes, he knows what to do with it.' With that, he was gone. We could only see the top of his head as it weaved and bobbed through cars.

When Babes came back, Tiny gave him the bottle of brandy. Babes took the bottle to an old battered car and hid it. After joining us, he said, 'I use that battered car as a store-room, and all these posh ones,' he said, waving his hand carelessly around, 'I use as sitting-rooms for my customers.

'You know, Duggie,' said Babes, 'if Shamba can go on at this rate for another year, he'll damn well buy his own car. He steals six to seven bottles a day, and when the store is busy, he steals up to a dozen.'

'What's the risk like?' asked Tiny.

'Not much risk, the way Shamba handles it. The funny-looking beads around his neck and the oversize overalls does the trick. Him being short also helps. You know all short men love clowning. There are days that Shamba leaves the baas and the whole staff roaring with laughter.

'His baas once asked about those strange beads around his neck. Shamba told the baas that it's a family custom. Meanwhile the necklace really acts as an anchor for the bottle that's hanging between his shoulder blades. The overalls hide the bulge. Every time they send him out, a full bottle goes with him. His baas once suggested he cut the overalls down to his own size. Shamba nearly fainted. "Baas!" he said, "my father will disown me! He didn't give me the overalls to cut, he gave them to me to wear. Besides, these overalls bring me luck." After that the white man didn't worry Shamba. He took him to be a little mad, otherwise a hard, solid worker.'

After the drink in the car, we left the car park, determined to go back to Sophiatown and to steal nothing on the way. To ensure this, we rammed our hands into our pockets and kept our eyes glued on to the pavement before us. As we crossed Main Street, someone in a khaki dustcoat with a duster rag in his hand paused from cleaning a shoe-shop window and greeted Tiny.

After walking on for a few yards, Tiny said, 'Will you believe it, Duggie, if I told you that the man we just saw cleaning the window back there doesn't work at that shop?' I nearly stopped in my tracks. Tiny said, 'Don't stop, man, walk on. . . . He works all the blocks in town dressed as he is: dustcoat and red duster. His name is Victor. He's what the Americans call a confederate trickster.'

'A confidence trickster,' I corrected.

'When he sees a likely victim admiring what's in a window, he'll move and start cleaning that window. After a few strokes with the duster he'll move in and say, "If you like that, I can get it for you. You see, I work here. If you want I can get it for you back-door at half price." It never fails, Duggie. Victor goes to the back of the shop. When he comes back, he'll be carrying a neatly-wrapped shoe box. The victim won't open the box for fear of getting Victor into trouble with his employers. Money will exchange hands. His victims are mostly domestic servants. When they reach wherever they're going, they find that they've just bought themselves something like a pair of old useless shoes. I don't care for such a profession, Duggie – it's too slimy for my liking. I prefer the open game. Like the gangster, the shop-lifter, even the smash-and-grabber. A life with no strings attached, no conscience-pricker. Something that needs no brains, you know what I mean, something like jazz that goes in the one ear and out the other. No regrets, no nothing. Like food you ate the previous day.

'But Victor's game, it's too classic. It has to be because it lives with you forever. It sticks to the subconscious mind like meat in pie. A future of "Brother, look over your shoulder!" The danger in this game, Duggie, lies in injured ego. Not the deed, but the principle will get you in the end. What greater provocation is there on earth than when you enter a human being's mind and start misplacing things? No living soul wants to be made a fool of.

'The success of every confed . . . I mean, confidence trickster depends upon cleverness. Cleverness that oozes from a brain that gets its stimulants from the vitamins of an empty stomach. It's like a game of snakes and ladders; the victim usually prefers the rungs to the ladders instead of the long and safe way around. Only to be swallowed by the snakes, emerging from its bowels with nothing to show but grief and misery.

'The seekers of manna from heaven are responsible for the con man's bulging waist-line, Duggie. If they ignore the shortcuts of life, they won't be touched. They should let the perspiration of their brows tighten their purse strings. Be deaf, and he'll never reach you, let alone touch you. Remember, his life depends upon explaining.'

'Tiny,' I said with awe, 'I didn't know you got education!'

After listening to Tiny, I started thinking deeply. I was mulling over what Tiny told me. Like Tiny, I didn't care much for such a game. In spite of that, that confidence trickster gave me an idea. An idea that could be made to work. All it needed was guts and brains. And I think I had them both.

The following day I went to the Indian market alone. I didn't want to tell Tiny my idea, in case it back-fired. At the market I bought a second-hand khaki overall. I took it to an Indian tailor shop. I instructed the Indian to sew the letters 'A.B.' on the shoulder-blades. The letters should be red. This is the uniform of the African staff at the A.B. Bazaar.

This bazaar is big. It boasts three storeys and a basement and about two to three hundred African workers. It's always packed with customers of all races, so it's only natural to see African labourers carrying goods about the place.

I spent one whole week studying the place from the inside. When I was sure of all angles, I donned my overalls and went to work. I wasn't a registered employee, but that did not worry me because I knew it.

I took advantage of two facts. One: to all whites a black man's features don't count. Only his colour does. To them, we are all alike; when you're black, you're just another black man. They don't even bother about your real name. To them, you're just John, Jim, or Boy. Your Daddy spends nine months thumbing through a dictionary for a fancy name to bestow on you and then some white trash comes and calls you what he feels like without even bothering to think or look at you. If that isn't contempt, then what is?

The second fact – and I like it best – is that they have a total disregard for our mental efficiency. That's why they couldn't dream that anyone, especially a black man, could be capable of doing what I did in this big bazaar.

If I took from the third floor, the staff there thought I was from the second floor. If I looted the basement they thought I was from the ground floor. A white assistant actually said to me in the basement department, 'Boy, leave that and help me here.'

If I carried the goods across town to Black Mischark's barber shop, the police thought I was a delivery boy. I was the only one who didn't think. It wasn't worth it. Not while everyone else did the thinking for me.

As time went on, things became even easier for me. I was getting accustomed to the place. I learned where to take and where not to take. Best of all, the staff, both black and white, took a liking to me. Hell, it looked as if I was going to get promotion. A few white sales ladies would send me out for sandwiches and cigarettes. I was a John-do-this, and a John-do-that. The only place I kept well away from was the pay-master's office. Hell, I'm not greedy. Fridays, when the boys queued for their pay, I was gone.

Good things never last, and they always seem to stop lasting on a Saturday.

'Stop thief!'

I froze. At last, I thought. When I looked back, I saw one of our European female workers frantically pointing at an African who was hurrying away with four boxes under his armpits.

'Stop thief! Stop him, John!' She was looking directly at me. When I hesitated, she said, 'Hurry, he's getting away.' I cursed the thief under my breath and made after him with every intention of letting him get away. Just as I was about to veer away at one of the entrances, two interfering white men caught him just as he was about to sprint through the street door.

'Here, boy, we got him for you.' I was going to ignore them when I became conscious of someone breathing down my neck. Looking back, I saw the floor manager breathing flames like a dragon; with him were two African workers. I was hemmed in between the floor manager and the thief catchers. There was nothing I could do. So I did the next best thing. I grabbed the thief.

There was fear in the African's eyes; he was shaking badly. I was shaking just as badly, but they must have thought that it was because I was holding him.

As we led the thief back to the manager's office, I sought for a way to get out of this awkward situation. I felt certain that once I entered that office my doom would be sealed.

Desperately, I reviewed my position, but everything looked hopeless. I stole a quick glance at the floor manager and saw him angrily grinding his teeth as he led the procession towards his office. Clearly this was no time for me to ask one of the African workers to hold the thief for me. Spectators made way for us and as we moved on our number swelled with officials and curious onlookers. You'd have thought we'd just caught a dangerous maniac. I saw my chances of getting away slip with every step we took.

As he opened the office door, he looked at me and growled, 'Don't lose him, or you lose your job.' I didn't mind. You can't lose what you haven't got. I just hate prison.

I pushed the thief roughly in, meaning to retreat, but someone pushed me in from behind and heeled the door shut. It was the second white man.

Putting up a bold front, I went to the closed door. My hand was closing around the knob when the floor manager paused, phone in hand, and said to the second white man, 'Don't think we didn't know.'

Oh God! So all the time he knew.

Turning to me he said, 'You stay right here and guard this kaffir.' The kettle and the pot are on the same stove, I thought. All sizzling equally. After that I was completely disregarded. It was as if me and the thief didn't exist.

There's nothing so gnawing and nerve-racking as uncertainty, especially if you're guilty. It's like hanging in mid-air with nothing holding you up. You know you're going to fall and break your neck. That's all right, you've half expected it. But what produces mental agony to a point of madness is this unseen thing that's holding you up. You wonder when it's going to snap. I was fast becoming a total nervous wreck.

There was a light tap on the door. Me and the thief both stiffened visibly. Instead of the expected police, the lady who served at the counter where the goods were stolen came in. She gave me a dazzling smile and the thief a dirty look.

'You want me, *mynheer?*' she asked, addressing herself to the floor manager.

'No, Miss Smith, you go back to your counter; I'll send for you when the time comes.' She turned and left the office, but not before flashing me another smile.

I was changing my weight to the other foot when my jaw itched violently. Before I could guess again, they came in. I don't know whether it's imagination, but every time I see a policeman, my jaw begins to itch violently. They didn't even knock, and I didn't have to guess their size. They were there. I felt my skin crawl.

'Boy!' the floor manager had to call me twice before I could swallow my fear.

'Boy, will you go and tell Miss Smith that the police are here.'

'Heh? Yes, baas.'

'Then come back here with her.'

I walked out of that office stiff-legged, as if I was leading a funeral procession. I couldn't believe such luck.

Then come back here, the man had said. What kind of fool did he take me to be? In pirate stories, once they make you walk the

63

plank, you don't walk it twice. Why should I? Once through that door, they never saw me again.

The day following that narrow escape, a white policeman riding a motor bike with a side car, called at Sisinyana's place looking for someone by the name of John. He was accompanied by an A.B. employee. When I heard this, I nearly left town. What kept me rooted was the fact that I was terribly short of money and Jeegar had a railway job lined up.

8

Me, Tiny and Jeegar were driving to the other side of Randfontein, where the lonely siding was situated. A distance of about forty miles lay ahead of us. Our road passed through Newlands where the biggest police station was situated. It was built just at the tail end of Sophiatown, buffering Sophiatown from Newlands.

The humming drone of the engine soothed my nerves, making me feel strangely elated. As the car drove on, I caught myself humming with the engine. Tiny was saying, 'Did you have trouble getting the car, Jeegar?'

Jeegar shook his head without taking his eyes from the road. He was the only one who could drive a car. Then without turning his head, he said, 'That Chinaman is too greedy to refuse. He'd sell his life for money.'

'What do the Chinese do with all the money they make?' asked Tiny. When nobody replied, he said, 'You'd think they live for nothing else but money, money, money.' To satisfy himself, he said loudly, 'Send it to China, I guess.'

'How could he refuse us his car after what we've already done for him?' Jeegar said, his eyes glued on the road. 'Besides,' he added, 'the agreement between us safeguards the bastard while we stand to fry both sides!'

'What do you mean by saying we fry both sides?' I asked, not realising that it was the same deal as Nine and me had organised. 'I hate burning.'

'Ask Tiny,' suggested Jeegar. I turned to Tiny.

'What does Jeegar mean by saying we fry both sides, Ti . . .'

'Look!' said Tiny excitedly.

From the side window of the car I saw a figure run out of a street crossing. It turned and raced in the same direction that we were travelling, keeping well on the side of the flat and straight road.

I tried to focus my eyes on the feet of the running figure, but found it almost impossible. The feet were moving too fast for the naked eye to follow. They were just a blur. I've never seen such fast-moving feet. Maybe there were wings attached to the ankles. They were just not touching ground. From the same crossing shot the nose of a pick-up van, nearly crashing into us. Jeegar cursed as he swerved to the right, narrowly avoiding an almost certain crash with a tramcar whose bells were shrieking ear-splitting warnings.

The police van was gaining on the winged figure. In all fairness they should have abandoned the chase and given the benefit of the doubt to the runner. The man was too damn good.

'Christ!' said Tiny, awed. 'You ever seen anything like this, Duggie?'

'No, but I'm seeing it now.'

'Know who that is?'

I nodded, I had recognised the ugly king-size pimples on his face as he took the corner at the crossing.

'It's brother Ortell, he sometimes patronises Sisinyana's she-been. He specialises in H.B. (House Breaking). Remind me to buy him a scale of skokiaan when next we meet,' said Tiny.

'If he sticks to this straight and narrow road, it will be a long time before you can buy him that scale,' prophesied Jeegar.

'Can't we pick him up?' I asked apprehensively, as I fingered my jaw.

'No,' said Jeegar. 'Definitely no! This job is not going to be spoilt by any gallant actions! Crime and chivalry don't mix.'

I lay back and continued to enjoy the ride. We were not going to hit the place until well after dark. To kill time, Jeegar left the white suburbs of Randfontein and drove the car to one of Randfontein's meanest-looking African townships. Guarding the gate at the main entrance of the township was a municipal policeman heavily armed with a spiked knob stick. Next to the big gate was the township superintendent's offices. We left the car and walked up to the offices where we were issued with twelve-hour visiting passes. These passes would shield us from arrest while in the township.

Jeegar nosed the car along the rutted streets. The streets were muddy and slimy because they were without gutters. They were strewn with dirty dish-water. The air reeked with overflowing latrines. Naked children with bloated bellies stood lined up, staring at us with mouths hanging open at this glimpse of glitter from the outside world. Now and again, braver ones would steal a ride on the back bumper of the car.

Jeegar turned a corner and stopped in front of a rain-rusted cottage. As we filed out of the car, women that were sitting long-legged on woven grass mats screamed with joy as they saw Jeegar. We filled ourselves with thick maize porridge and drank it down with a brew known as Black Courage. There's very little difference between skokiaan and Black Courage. The only difference lies in the name. To me, the stuff tastes the same, and both are equally sinful.

This Black Courage not only made us a little drunk, it also ran true to form. It gave us the necessary courage for the job ahead.

The goods train was emptied without a hitch. Jeegar drove back to the cottage at Randfontein. We didn't think it wise for us to proceed to Johannesburg at that time of the night as we were almost certain to run into the night patrols. So we decided to pull out of Randfontein at the first light of dawn.

That night the zinc cottage vibrated with noise as we celebrated. There was a four-gallon tin of Black Courage, plus a bottle of Tambo Lenyoka ('Snake Bone'), a colourless liquid made from the vapour of boiling corn. I don't remember leaving the cottage or being carried to the car.

The wind cutting into the side window and the painful hunched position that I found myself in must have been responsible for bringing me out of my drunken stupor.

My shirt smelt of vomit. I moved my legs, and felt a wetness. God, I had wet my own bloody trousers.

The taste in my mouth was revolting. It was as if I had been

66

feeding on rotten intestines. My tongue felt thick and scurvy. I wanted to open my mouth to let it hang out, it was taking up too much space. My fingers were shaking uncontrollably, while disgust and loathing for myself mounted by the minute. God! What a hangover!

'Don't you think we should abandon the car?' It was Tiny talking. There was anxiety in his voice.

'No!' came from Jeegar. 'Not after all the trouble we've gone through. We might still make it.'

'But you yourself have admitted that time has run out on us, that we overslept.'

'We might still make it!' insisted Jeegar irritably.

After that, there was silence in the car except for the steady drone of the engine and the ceaseless hammering pain in my head.

Suddenly Tiny shouted with an unusual trace of panic in his voice, 'No! No! Jeegar, look at the time, we'll never make it, man! Stop the car and let me out – you can have my share of the goods. Only for God's sake stop the car and let me out!'

'Shut up and sit still, and keep your hands off the steering wheel – do you want to kill us all?'

I looked around for the first time and wondered about Tiny's sudden outburst. It was not like him. Besides, nothing seemed to have gone wrong. Our car was still packed to capacity. Through the small back window I saw no sign of approaching trouble. Why should Tiny run up a sweat? The answer wasn't long in coming. As if by magic, we found ourselves sardined between two squad cars.

I looked through my side of the window and saw a red face grinning at me. The other squad car signalled to Jeegar to pull up. There was nothing he could do. The cards were up. They had us cold. Tiny was shouting, 'I told you! I told you! Damn you! I told you!' Right on the car's floorboards I bent my head and was violently sick.

It's very vague, but I recall being driven into the yard of Newlands police station and pushed into the charge office. A charge was read but I was too dense or dazed to understand. Then we were ushered through a passage that led to the cells at the back. As the turn-key opened the iron gate, he said to Tiny, 'This one stinks like the crevices of a witch doctor's buttocks after an initiation ceremony. What's the matter with him, is this his first lock-up?'

That night in the cell, Jeegar was cursing the Chinaman with every foul word that he could lay his tongue on. I didn't think it right. After all, it was just our bad luck that landed us there. Jeegar was cursing the Chinaman, Tiny was cursing Jeegar and I was cursing my weakness for drink.

'When we awoke at the Randfontein cottage, you told me yourself that time had run out on us. Go on, deny it, go on!'

'Shut up, Tiny,' Jeegar said.

'I won't shut up, Jeegar! The trouble with you is that you are born greedy. Always was, and always will be. I'm saying it here and now, and I'll always say it – if you had listened to me and not your greed, we would have jumped the fire and remained with our freedom. We wouldn't be here. No! Never! I repeat, we wouldn't be here.'

I wished Tiny would shut up. He was putting more strain on my strained nerves. Didn't he realise I was dying?

'Tiny,' I said at last, 'will you for God's sake shut up?'

He ignored me and continued to revile Jeegar, who was now engaged in the task of carefully turning his pockets inside-out in the hope of finding cigarette waste. All our possessions had been taken from us, including our cigarettes and matches.

'You knew the rules,' went on Tiny. 'But you ignored them.'

Nursing his find carefully in the palm of his hand, Jeegar said, 'What would you be saying if we had made it?'

'Don't talk shit, Jeegar. The Chinaman was to report his car stolen to the police at exactly seven o'clock, and where were we at that time? Right in Randfontein under dirty blankets!'

Jeegar cursed. 'I still think that bloody Chink could have waited for another hour.'

'What! And run the risk of losing his car?

'Wasn't the agreement that he lends us his car for the job and if we were not back by seven o'clock he reports the car stolen to the police? If he had given us that extra hour that you're raving about, and we were found with the goods, he would have been taken as an accomplice and his car would have been confiscated. Besides, we promised to abide by the rules, and an agreement is an agreement, even if it's made with a Chinaman.'

68

'You'll never make a successful criminal, Tiny,' growled Jeegar.

'Not if I tag along with you!' Tiny yelled. 'What we should have done was to hide the goods and abandon the car at the stroke of eight, like that Cinderella picture.'

'I still say . . .'

'Shut up, Jeegar, you make me sick! You heard what that charge sheet read. Instead of one sheet, there are two.

'One reads, "Theft from the railways", instead of just plain theft. Do you know what that means? To them, this is special. They are going to charge us with every undetected crime that ever took place on the railways in the hope that we were the gang responsible. That alone's worth a five- to seven-year sentence – they are going to throw the book at us, Jeegar!

'The second charge sheet reads . . .'

'Shut up!' screamed Jeegar, getting to his feet.

Tiny jeered and went on, 'The second charge reads, "Car theft". It should read "car theft by arrangement", but it doesn't, for the simple and logical reason that the Chinaman will never admit his part in the deal. In fact, to him we just don't exist! So stop clenching your fists and spilling those cigarette grains and tell us about the penalties that go with car theft. Let your previous convictions be your guide!' Then Tiny did a surprising thing. He sat flat on his buttocks and cried bitterly.

While all this was going on, I was listening with a detached mind, then my brains started revolving slowly. I wanted very much to detach them again, but what Tiny said about two charges when I only knew of one made it difficult. I could excuse the railway charge, but it also said car theft. I knew nothing about that. I didn't steal any car, nor did I know about Chinaman arrangements.

That night I slept very little. The cell was lousy with lice. I thanked the Almighty when the first signs of daylight filtered through the cell window. I studied my surroundings. The first thing I saw was the sleeping figure of a man, covered from head to foot with these foul blankets. He slept as if he was in a nursery. Must be a bigger louse, I concluded. My hangover was much better, in fact it was almost gone. I felt that I might live. Even if I stank like a Zulu warrior's armpits.

Jeegar got up. He went to all the prisoners in the cell, about fifteen in all. He started kicking, cursing and pulling the blankets roughly from them. The lion is back in his jungle, I thought. A guard peeping through the iron bars grinned his approval.

He went to the prisoner who was covered from head to foot, and whisked the blanket off. The figure groaned.

'Hey, Duggie,' yelled Jeegar. 'Know who this one is? It's our friend with the flying feet – Ortell! Just look where that straight and narrow road led him! Look at him!' He laughed. 'They've buggered him up good and solid. He's all bruised and bashed up – he can't even see!' I took a look at Ortell. He was mumbling unintelligible sounds.

The iron gate clanked open. Tiny said, 'Fall in next to me, Duggie. We are on the way to Number Four.'

'What about him?' I asked glancing at the inert form of Ortell.

'Forget about him,' said Jeegar. 'He's not going anywhere. They won't take the chance of making him appear before a magistrate or doctor while he's in that condition! He'll lie here until he's fully healed before they lay a charge against him.'

Number Four. The Fort. A prison dug out of a mountain as far back as the turn of the last century. It's a mile from the heart of Johannesburg City. Its bold, hideous structure makes the surrounding suburbs look ugly. Like a septic boil on the face of a beautiful girl.

As I shuffled through the giant gates, a ghoulish feeling started engulfing me. A feeling you would get when you invaded the bowels of an ancient tomb. A cracking sound that could only have been produced by a pistol or whip in the hands of an expert made me forget all about ghouls and tombs. But neither whip nor pistol was responsible for the cracking sound. It was the palm of an open hand landing with force on an unprotected face.

The smack was dealt out by a Blue Jacket convict trustee. A Blue Jacket is a convict who served indefinitely. It may be seven, it may be fifteen years. It all depends on the prison board members.

Criminals are in dread of this sentence, because it doesn't terminate. The least you are expected to serve is seven years if your behaviour is good. I'd like to see the results of good behaviour if a man finds himself locked up in a cage with a pack of hyenas. Besides, I don't see how anyone can be good in jail, when he's there because he's been bad. . . .

Smack! 'Answer fast, you black bastard, where do you think you are? In your mother's womb?'

The newcomer stood naked while his belongings were checked.

'One trouser, baas, one shirt, one pair boots, no socks, one cap, baas, no money, no watch, no nothing.' Smack! 'Move, dog!' He recited all this in one breath.

'Next! Name!' Smack! 'Don't stammer, you dog! Father's name? Which river do you drink from? Which tribe do you belong to? What's the name of your chief?'

You've got to answer fast, be bright and awake all the time. If you are dull-witted, you enter the big cell bleeding. The Dutch clerk sitting behind the counter took all this down without lifting his head.

After three months waiting trial, while they were searching for our previous convictions, we were hauled in front of a magistrate. Tiny was right. He threw the book at us. I got five years' hard labour plus ten strokes; Tiny got the same. Jeegar was sentenced to seven years' imprisonment because of his previous convictions.

9

I was in a span of forty; each of us had diffferent sentences, ranging from twenty years to five. Not one of us was a fourteen. A fourteen is a convict who serves one to two years or even less. We were leaning on the handles of our pickaxes, resting from the gruelling task of having to drive a pickaxe into hard, rocky earth. We were making tar-road gravel. I had long stopped trying to fight the sweat that was running freely down my face.

'Chocholoza!' Chocholoza is the song that South African blacks sing under hardship. Especially by long-term convicts when engaged in hard labour. Chocholoza is like a child with no parents. Nobody knows when or where it originated from, but

71

what everyone knows is that when there is some kind of deep-rooted ache in the heart the first thing to visit the lips will be 'Chocholoza'. The song with no beginning and no end, as old as misery itself.

This mystery song of dark ages was passed down to us by our ancestors through generations of hardship. Its sound rises from the very depths of a tortured soul. It encourages faith to take up when hope threatens to leave off. The word *Chocholoza* means 'Go forward' or 'Make way for the next man'.

'Chocholoza!' The convicts in the first row were beginning to sing in high-pitched, almost soprano voices. This was the cue for the rest of us to lift our pickaxes high above our heads in one smooth motion and hold them suspended in mid-air. The more experienced convicts would twist the handles of the picks with one deft movement of the wrist, causing the two sharp points to blur as one in the air. Then they held them poised for the earthward drive.

The bass voices repeated: 'Chocholoza!' The signal to strike. The pickaxes came down swiftly in one smooth motion like conducted lightning bolts piercing the stubborn ground with a forty-in-one sound.

'Kwezantaba!' (At those far away mountains). Up went the axes to remain poised in the air, waiting for the bass voices to repeat the word 'Kwezantaba' before coming down in rhythmical precision.

I wished they wouldn't hold the song out so long when the pickaxes were in mid-air. My arms couldn't carry the weight too long. Clearly this was no place for weaklings. I wondered how Tiny was making out.

The singing went on: 'Wena uya goloza'. (You're a cheeky man). The bass voices would echo the words. 'Goba uya baleka'. (Because you're running away.) The bass voices repeat . . .

'Chocholoza!' God! Is this how I was to spend five years of my life?

'Chocholoza!'

To hell with the song, it was doing nothing to help my aching muscles. As for my heart, it was about to stop beating and no amount of singing was going to stand in its way. I checked around at my immediate surroundings. I didn't know why I was doing it, but what I did know was that it wasn't with the intention of escaping. That was out of the question.

This was no reformatory. This was the real thing: prison; ten rifles, fifteen assegais, all placed strategically on high ground. Each convict was under direct focus. These Afrikaner guards didn't smell green. One stood, spread-legged directly above me, cradling his rifle like it was his only child. He kept throwing abusive language in the short-cut Zulu language known as Fanakalo. His words were very discouraging. He kept saying. 'Ten years jele no skuff two week, faka lo nstimbi lo pick lo shovel' – Ten years prison life with no food for two weeks, put you in irons with a pick and shovel. 'Three months kululute pikanin skuff, zonke lem tondo yena fele hazeko lom fazi, nyansi nkosi pezulu' – Three months in the kulukutes. The kulukutes are the small torture cells. Pikannin skuff means food fit for a small boy. *Zonke lom tomdo yene fele* means all the sexual organs will be dead through lack of womanly comforts, true as there is a God above.

As he came to the part of deadly sexual organs, I couldn't help grinning. Not when one long-term convict had already tried his luck on me. I had an uneasy feeling that I was going to have to fight like hell to keep these romping sexual organs out of my thighs. If they used direct methods, it would have been easy to fight them off. But those dogs were sly. To make you a 'boy', that's the prison term for woman, they first tried the direct approach. That meant asking you outright. If you show bared teeth, they began to bribe you.

The convict who favoured you would first give you a much-needed puff from his rolled tobacco. He'd see to it that you were well-fed, he'd make sure to get you the best prison garb and regular pieces of meat. By meat I mean pork fat.

If you were a fool, you'd think he was being friendly. There's no such thing as friendship in prison. Nobody comes to prison for the purpose of making friends. Here only survival counts. The only sure way to survival lies on top of the shoulders of the next man. Here dog eats dog. The prison-wise ignore such clock-precision gifts. A time will come when you can't do without these regularities. Then the old-timers move in and you are ready to be slaughtered. You become a regular mistress. Your morals are torn to shreds. You need all the physical strength you have to protect your morals. You have to fight till you drop. Mother Nature can always rebuild your physique, but morals you have to shape yourself. That all takes will-power, something I'm sadly in need of.

There was a newcomer in my cell, nice plump and juicy-looking – the way I like my girls to look. His buttocks wobbled under his short pants when he walked, his fat thighs shone as if smeared with fat.

The convicts took one look at the boy, then started tearing at one another. Not me.

The hooter blasted, giving out a shrill sound that drowned out my guard's abusive ravings. We were through for the day. When the hooter sounded off, it meant we had at least worked off one day of our sentence. One after the other the convicts would yell, depending on their sentences. One who had served two years of his twenty, would yell, 'Woza eighteen years!' (Come eighteen years); the one who had served three out of his ten would yell, 'Come seven years!'

It was heart-breaking to hear them urging the years to come nearer. Somehow, it helped. I drew courage from those that still had a long way to go.

'Come five!' I shouted. Unlike the other convicts there wasn't much heart in my shouting. It sounded faint and feeble. I'm sure there was a kind of sob in it. Anyway, I was the last to admit to such weakness.

My five came, hard.

After my visit to the Fort, I was in and out of prisons as if I had a share in them. The place becomes a magnet once you've graced it with your presence. With the records I piled up, I was a regular prison fan. All theft records!

The funny thing is, I didn't for one minute think that there could be any other kind of life for me except this kind. I just accepted it. Stealing to me was – well, just living.

Three months out of Cinderella Prison and I was hauled before a magistrate again. He took it upon himself to look at me with disgust. I didn't care. After all, the man was not my redeemer.

He actually stood on his feet as he declared me society's number one pest. A habitual criminal with slimy ambitions, something that should be stamped out, and if he didn't send me away for a long time, he'd be failing in his duty not only to society but to God as well. I wanted to tell him that the trouble with him was that he took his job too seriously. But the man was too angry. It would only have made him more dangerous and mean. He looked at the pile of documents before him, then he pushed them aside as if they'd contaminate him. He drummed his fingertips on the desk. He seemed to be pondering. This man was overworked.

He picked up the first document and after studying it, looked at me. I was feeling hungry. Speaking almost as if to himself he said, 'Five years at the Fort. Theft!' Throwing it aside, he picked up another, 'Nine months Leeukop Prison, theft! Eighteen months Bobbejaan Spoor, theft! Six months Cinderella Prison, theft! Eighteen months Sonderwater Prison, theft!' He snorted.

Thinking that he was wasting his time by going carefully through all the documents, he hurriedly thumbed through them muttering. 'Theft, theft, theft – *Got!*' There was saliva at the corner of his lips, 'What kind of a creature are you?'

'It was all for food, my baas.'

'Food?' There was contempt in his voice. 'I'm going to send you to where you are going to get it three times a day, and if you do not come back, it will be God's will.' Grinning, he looked skywards as if whispering secretly to God. I didn't like that. God knows.

'How long have you been outside?'

'Three months.' The prosecutor interrupted, whispering something to the magistrate. Two against one, I thought.

He looked at me and smiled. There was irony in the smile. The same kind of smile landed Napoleon on some island.

Clearing his throat he said, 'I was going to give you an indeterminate sentence, but you can thank the prosecutor for suggesting something quite different and worthwhile. It so happens that there's a war on. I don't think you knew, did you?' I didn't. How could I? I had a private war of my own, the fight for existence.

'This country needs soldiers. You can choose between joining the army or being sent to prison indefinitely.

Blackmail sprinkled with justice, I thought. He knew damn

well that the scars of Blue Sky were still fresh in my mind, and here he was threatening to send me back. 'Blue Sky' is the unofficial name for Cinderella Prison, because that's all you see. The sky and nothing else.

'The army!' I almost shouted, but held myself. It should be easier to run from there than from the 'Sky'.

IO

The year 'forty. The white men were desperately in need of soldiers. They were recruiting black men foul or fair – mostly foul – forcing them to go and put on a fire they didn't help kindle. Unemployment flourished on purpose; not that I wanted to be employed. It became a matter of join the army or starve. Every morning men would go looking for work, only to come back carrying long faces. Homes went to pieces. Women had to leave them to go and whore in order to maintain their offspring.

In the Native Military Corps there were two things that disgusted me. First the kind of food they gave us; it wasn't fit for a dog. Second, we were not allowed the use of rifles. Not even to clean. They armed us with assegais. There's nothing wrong with the assegai provided the nation we were going to fight – they referred to them as Germans – were also going to use spears. Bringing down an aeroplane with the aid of a spear, was something I was going to live for. Even the cotton wool in my head told me that there was something terribly wrong with this assegai business.

This was my third month in the army plus one week A.W.O.L. I was lying low in Sisinyana's shebeen wondering how to escape punishment. The military police were all over the place. I'd long since discovered that getting out of the army and staying out for good was next to impossible. Not with a magistrate waiting for me in civilian life.

I was drinking skokiaan with two other soldiers, all deserters. One was a Coloured in the Cape Corps.

Victor the ex-con man was saying, 'You worry about being

absent without leave for one week only? Why don't you do what I once did – play dumb! I once stayed away from camp for three weeks, sleeping with another soldier's wife. When I finally got back, I purposely went to the wrong camp and made myself at home there. The next morning, after dismissing roll call, I went up to the sergeant and asked why he never called my name after roll call. He gave me a scornful look and demanded my name. Respectfully I told him my name, number and rank. After going through all the names on his list, he frowned.

'"Why the hell isn't your name here?"

'"I don't know, Sarge."

'"Where the hell are you from?" he barked.

'"This is my third week here, Sarge."

'"I don't want to know how long you've been here, what I want to know is, where were you stationed before you came here?"

'"I was stationed at Welgedacht, Sarge."

'"How did you come here?"

'"By train, Sarge."

'"You mean you were not transferred to this camp officially?"

'"I don't know what you mean by the word officially, Sarge, but seeing that all soldiers are the same, and therefore brothers in arms, fighting the same enemy and for the same cause, I didn't see anything wrong in coming to this camp, so I just chose the nearest camp and came to it. You see, I didn't have enough train fare to go to my original camp."

'"Where's your kit?"

'"Back where I was, Sarge, that is if it's not already stolen. I thought you people will issue me with a new one."'

Wiping the skokiaan foam from his thick lips, Victor continued, 'The sergeant's face swelled up right in front of me. I never knew human beings could produce sounds like dying frogs. In the meantime I had sold boots, bush-jacket, great coat and ground sheet to Sisinyana. She had bought the stuff for one of her hole-diggers.'

'What happened to you?' I asked Victor.

'Nothing,' he said, belching. 'The sergeant hauled me before the commanding officer and did all the talking for me.

'"Look at this bloody block-headed private," he howled. "Will we ever make good fighting soldiers out of these black idiots? You haul one foot out of the bush and the bastard puts in the other. He's been lying in this camp for three weeks because he thought that it didn't make any difference in which camp he was as long as it's a soldiers' camp. He's originally from Welgedacht!" All the C.O. said was, "Take him to the adjutant's office and have them make out a report then send him back to his camp with the first mail truck!"'

I grinned. I wasn't grinning at Victor's experience. I was remembering something about him.

The reason why Victor joined the assegai force is because he suffered from bad memory. It's bad for a con man to have a bad memory. He told me so himself. He complained that he was looking too much over his shoulder, that his memory was so bad that it was difficult to remember who his victims were. A good con man should have a camera mind, so as to spot before being spotted.

Victor had conned so many flat-boy Zulus, that it was dangerous for him to walk the streets without meeting one of them. And Zulus have a habit, call it dirty if you like, of fighting at the drop of a hat. They never forgive a wrong.

His last job was what made him hurriedly put his name on a recruiting pad. He was selling a perfume to the Zula flat-boys.

His perfumes were guaranteed to make any white housewife fall madly in love with her black servant. The master was in danger of losing the madam to his native servant. One whiff, and her parachute won't open. She'll just fall, and fall and fall. No need to go into detail about how the flat-boys queued for this ninth-wonder-of-the-world perfume. Victor in the army was enough proof of that.

But I had my own worries. How to get back to camp or how to get out of the army for good. Victor told me one way of how to beat the guard room and escape pack drill, but that was one man's meat, it might not have worked out that way for me.

'Duggie.' It was the Coloured soldier. 'Are you people really being issued with assegais instead of rifles?'

I nodded miserably. 'That's nothing, you should see the food they give us. Potatoes, pumpkins, carrots, tomatoes – not one of them peeled! All dumped into the same pot with the meat. The

78

pot is lined with motor-car grease – it must be car grease because that's how it tastes! I'm not going back there! And what really boils my bile is the speech I heard over the wireless! The General said we natives are not going to be rewarded with money after the war because we don't know the use of money. Our reward will be cattle. I've long given up trying to think of what use a cow will be to me! They say you Coloured soldiers will be given money because you know what to do with it. I happen to know that the only money a Coloured knows anything about is liquid money – and that's a fact!'

The Coloured soldier laughed.

'In the C.C.,' he said, 'we get good food, good uniforms, and we are issued with rifles. We even get more money than the N.M.C.'

'That's because they're your uncles,' I cut in bitterly.

Then something Jeegar once said came to me. His actual words were, 'If you are in trouble and want to disappear from the police or anyone, never leave town or run. That's what any fool would do. The wisest thing is to blend with the local colour. Become part of the surrounding scenery.'

At first I didn't understand him, nor do I think anybody would have. Surely the best way to look after yourself is to run or keep out of sight? Now here was Jeegar telling me that in order to lose yourself you should look belonging, like one of the babies in the row of cots. It was only when he explained a little further that I began to understand.

Jeegar once got an indeterminate sentence, and while serving it at a place called Barberton in the Eastern Transvaal he eluded his guards and escaped. They searched for him all over the place, including Johannesburg, until they finally gave up.

Meanwhile, he was in another jail under a different name serving a six-month sentence for a minor offence. Who would have thought of looking for him in prison? Jeegar wasn't in the shade, he was in the branch that provided the shade.

The following morning I was in front of the Coloured Recruiting Office dressed as a civilian. I hardly had any trouble getting in. My Afrikaans is flawless, and my surname didn't need changing. Boetie means anything; mostly it means nothing.

While the military police were looking for me all over

Sophiatown, I was speeding towards Kimberley, my first Coloured base camp. The days of the spear went out of date with the last Zulu war at Blood River. Even then the damn things were no good. If I was going to fight any war, it was going to be with real weapons.

It was the biggest blunder of my life. I might still have been home drinking Sisinyana's skokiaan instead of inhaling desert sand into my throat through my nostrils as a transport driver in Garawi. I got there and back so fast that the thought still sends me reeling. It was Kimberley, Durban, then North Africa. Somebody was in a hurry for me to die.

The first night, a Friday, I was standing awed by the beauty of the desert. A soft breeze was blowing from the east, across sand dunes that stretched as far as I could see. In the moonlight they looked like a dead white sea.

On that Sunday, me and Private Penny Myburgh had to fetch the camp's weekly supply of rum. The drive in the merciless heat made us wish for all kinds of drinks.

The heat made Private Myburgh say, as we were driving back to camp with the supply, 'Christ, Duggie, my throat is dry.'

'Mine, too,' I affirmed.

There was a pause, then, 'Can't we pinch a little of the rum at the back?'

I shook my head. 'No chance – no tools. The barrels are heavily sealed.'

I stole a glance at Penny and saw his eyebrows screwing up, almost meeting the hairline. Heavy thinking, I thought; he's not going to get much opposition from me, not with Sisinyana's skokiaan uppermost in my mind.

'Stop the truck, Duggie.' He was wetting his lips by rubbing them together. His Adam's apple behaved like a yo-yo.

I ground to a stop. We got out of the truck and made for the back. One look at those formidable barrels told me that no race on earth could open them without the necessary tools. But I hadn't reckoned with the Coloured race: he's many races all in one. Nothing short of a wall of flame was going to stop Penny from getting a drink from one of those barrels. He raced to the dashboard of the truck and reappeared with a hammer and a nail.

Without a glance at me he punched a hole in the side of the barrel.

The rum pissed out.

'No cup,' I said.

'Hell, who wants a cup?' he said as he threw himself flat on his back, mouth open.

I gave him a few seconds then kicked him aside and went under. Then he kicked me aside, then I kicked him aside, then he kicked me aside. . . .

Then I remember being behind the wheel, doing a crazy zig-zag and laughing my head off with old Penny screaming beside me. Then there were all kinds of other noises and all kinds of other things all over the show. Hot lead noises, hot lead things and mushrooms of white sand shooting up around us. I remember Penny and me screaming together, but not with laughter anymore.

And then there was burning and blackness and silence. A long blackness and a long silence.

Nobody ever complained about the rum.

I I

Three months later, after my neat weekend stint as a desert rat, I was hanging on a pair of crutches like wet overalls on a washing-line. I was sailing home from the port of Aden. There were premature grey hairs on my head. My left leg was amputated above the knee, leaving a five-inch stump. But when I disembarked at Durban Docks, my stump had grown to below the knee. There were a dozen Belgium brownies reposing in my stump sock, my winnings at a dice school during the voyage. A man has to live.

By the time we got to Durban, my stump was paining me. It had taken a terrible beating from the artillery that was stored there. My first problem was to find a hiding-place for my winnings. It wasn't difficult. After wrapping them in a respect-able-looking parcel I took them to the Methodist Institute of

Soldiers at Grey Street, where I gave them to the reverend to keep until I called.

After getting rid of my armoury, I saw that my stump was bruised and swollen. This worried me. I reported it to the M.O. and, instead of going through with the troop train to Johannesburg, I was admitted to the Addington Hospital. It was through the social workers that I was fitted with a metal leg. The Army was all for giving me a wooden peg leg, but the social workers pointed out that such a leg would be too heavy for a five-inch stump. So I got a shiny new metal one, which I nearly lost.

That happened at Umbilo Park, after the orthopaedic people had fitted me with it. They advised me to take the leg to a place where there was a lot of grass to try it out, so that, when I fell, the grass would cushion me. I did. I chose Umbilo Park. I was giving myself a rest from the trying task of having to learn to walk all over again. It was painful work. My stump was getting all bruised up again, so I took the leg off to relieve the ache; and then I must have dozed off. When I woke up, the leg was gone. At first I thought the leg had walked off, but I ruled that out. It still couldn't walk properly. After searching fruitlessly for it, I decided to report the theft.

I was just hopping out of the park gate when I saw a one-legged hobo running away with it. The funny thing was that his right leg was amputated, as opposed to my left. Under his armpit dangled my artificial leg. The fool was going to end up having two left legs. I tried to give chase, but saw the uselessness of it. The bastard had the advantage of a crutch. I had none.

A few hours after that, the social workers drove me back to the scene of the crime. There, on the park bench, lay my immortal leg. A note was attached to it. On the note was written: 'Wrong side leg'. I could have told him, the son of a bitch.

Anyhow, after mastering the shine out of my brand new leg, I entrained for Johannesburg, armed with a letter from the social workers of Durban to those of Johannesburg. But not before collecting my armour from the reverend. Even priests can sometimes be put to good use.

I decided to give up my past life of being lean and free. I wanted to be fat and chained. I wanted to be an honest-to-God hard worker.

At Johannesburg the social workers got me a clerical job. If putting letters into envelopes can be termed clerical.

We were driving through the streets of Johannesburg in the firm's van. I was sitting at the back of the van while the white driver occupied the driver's seat. He was taking me to the pass-office where I was going to get my first pass. Without the white man's company it could have taken me as long as three weeks to get fixed up. And without the necessary pass, you were not allowed to work.

'Name?'

Just like Number Four, only here an Afrikaner asked the questions with rudeness equal to a convict trustee.

'Duggie,' I told him.

He paused to look at me. Then, 'From which fish-tin label did your father copy that name?'

The Afrikaans driver who had come with me doubled over with laughter. I swallowed and transferred my weight on to my artificial leg. I was getting tired of standing.

When he was through, he directed us to another office upstairs. We went into so many offices that my head whirled. In the last office we came to, a young clerk was chatting gaily to a European lady. When he saw us he became all business. I passed my papers through to him.

'Name?' It was right there in front of him.

'Duggie,' I said thickly, fearing another wisecrack.

'Ooh!' cooed the lady. 'That's my father's name.'

The devil came up in me. I couldn't, oh no, I just couldn't miss this chance. This was a coincidence that happens once in a million. To hell with the consequences.

Straightfaced, I blurted, 'From which fish-tin label did your grandfather copy that name?'

Knuckles like motor-bike ball-bearings crashed into my ribs, doubling me up. My balance stick fell; blindly I groped for it. I straightened up and started sucking great gulps of air into my tortured lungs.

'Know who you're speaking to, you black bastard!' It was my driver. I didn't look at him in case he might see what was in my eyes. Back in the van, I studied my black-stained fingers. I had

83

been fingerprinted so many times that it would take days before the stuff could be removed.

Through the mirror the driver saw me inspecting my stained fingers. He laughed outright, the one-sided humorous bastard.

I was serious about my job and stayed that way for about two years. I loved it. Then one day that devil came up again. It was the end of the month, one of our European female clerks called me into her office; an elderly lady with a nice homely face.

'Duggie,' she said, 'I'm lunching out today. Please have this packet of sandwiches.'

There was a big piece of ox-tongue reposing in my stomach. I was filled to the brim. Still, I felt it would be rude if I refused this kind lady's offer. And one day when there wouldn't be any ox-tongue weighing me down, she might not take it upon herself to help me out. I thanked her and took the packet to my office. I checked on my wrist-watch and saw that it was five minutes after one. Unconsciously I picked up the lunch packet and made for the street door. To get there I had to cross a big hall of working desks.

On my left was the secretary's office. It had a glass partition. You can see in from outside. I looked, and there was the secretary, Mr Groenewald. He was busy with the morning paper, both his feet were on his desk.

Without a thought, I knocked and went in.

'Mr Groenewald,' I said, placing the packet of sandwiches on his desk. 'Here's some sandwiches for you. I don't feel like anything today.'

With that, I went out. I didn't think a reply was necessary. The dials on my watch were on two-thirty when my internal phone rang. It was Colonel Pringle, head of the department. I was wanted upstairs.

What I saw when I entered his office made me uneasy. There, sitting like stone marble, was Mr Groenewald. My eyes travelled from him to the large desk.

Then I saw them. I was reminded of old times in court rooms. The exhibit, I mean the packet of sandwiches. There was black anger on Mr Groenewald's face.

Then someone coughed, or rather cleared his throat. It was the colonel.

'Duggie.'

'Yes, sir,' I stammered.

Again he coughed. 'Eh . . .' he started. 'Well –' again he coughed. He gave me the impression that he didn't know where to start. 'Well, damn it!' he exploded. 'Why did you give Mr Groenewald a packet of sandwiches?'

'Did I do wrong?'

'Well, damn it, no, but . . .' he coughed again as if his throat wasn't already cleared. 'You are not supposed to give a white man your food.'

'But . . .' I started. With a wave of his hand he shut me up.

'You should have taken the sandwiches upstairs to the building boys instead of giving them to Mr Groenewald. You have made him feel small.'

'Doesn't Mr Groenewald eat sandwiches?' I asked innocently. Hell, at war we used to eat out of the same dixie.

'No! I mean, yes, he does eat sandwiches, but not when they come from a . . .'

'Kaffir!' put in Mr Groenewald.

Indignantly I said, 'The sandwiches did not come from me, they came from Mrs Surge. I didn't feel like eating either, so I passed them to Mr Groenewald. What is wrong in that, sir?'

'Plenty,' growled Mr Groenewald. 'Who the hell do you think you are that you should come to my office and give me sandwiches? Do I look hungry to you?'

'No, I merely looked upon it as a gesture of humanity.'

Soothingly the colonel said, 'You should know, my boy, that it is not correct for a black man to give . . .'

'Not correct, sir?' I asked aghast.

'All right, damn you, get out of here.'

God! What a race! Unlike the black man, they are supposed to have had the advantage of a civilised environment, yet their barbarism is as thinly veiled as the prison lash strokes on my buttocks. I should have resigned on the spot, but determinedly I kept on. Then Mr Groenewald took it upon himself to make my life so miserable, that I was forced to resign two weeks after my misplaced kindness.

In 1948 the Nationalist Government came into power.

There was a big new building at 80 Albert Street. It was simply known as Influx Control. A beehive of black misery. They should have named it Liberty Control. This is where you had to report without the slightest delay after losing or resigning from a job. Failing which, you risked being charged under the Section 29 law, a law carrying a two-year jail sentence.

The trouble with this house of lawful humiliation is that here you are made to take any job they offer, whether it suits you or not. Here, black man must take work, not choose work. Remember, never talk back to your employer; you are not indispensable. You're in orbit around town. Don't accept employment twelve miles out of town, even if there's no work to be found where you live; you can lose, or forfeit, all right to live where you've always lived. Do not marry a girl who comes from a similar distance because she is regarded as a foreigner; they won't allow you to live together. If you want to visit relatives, see that your pass is properly stamped. Also, if you want to make some sort of celebration at your home, do not buy live-stock to slaughter without getting a special permit from the superintendent. Most important of all, before going to bed at night, make sure that your pass book is either in the pocket of the trousers or the jacket you're going to wear the following morning.

Influx Control was my destination. I was going there with the hope of getting new employment. As I approached the place, I nearly turned back. Queues a half-mile long were snaking around the four-block building. The Africans were moving in pairs at a snail's pace. Misery was written on every face, as if they were walking the last mile. Maybe we were, who knew. Most of us were either going to be given twenty-four hours to leave the urban area of Johannesburg, or sold to potato farmers for failing to renew work-seeking permits in time.

In time? Look at that queue! By the time I reached the small gate so as to get the necessary rubber stamp in my pass book, it would be four-thirty, time for them to close, making me twelve hours behind schedule and liable for arrest by any street policeman who demanded to see my pass.

There's a tall tale about the trees of Canada. They say the trees are so high that if you look straight up, it will take you three weeks to see the top. Right here in Johannesburg is a queue like that. Every time you came to that gate, it would be four-thirty.

Then they closed it in your face. If you tried to get back by five in the morning, you'd find that hundreds had had the same idea. If you spent the night there so as to be first in the morning, you risked arrest for Night Special.

Instead of joining the queue at the tail end, I made a beeline for the side-entrance. Imagine having to stand in a queue the whole day with only one leg to support you. Clearly this was no place for cripples, respectable or otherwise. The side entrance was guarded by two municipal police, commonly known as Black Jacks because of their black uniforms. You were not allowed to stand on the pavements. The pavement was for Europeans only. Europeans who were looking for servants, or those who were trying to get their servants' passes in order.

'What do you want? Why don't you join the queue?' asked the Black Jack glaring at me.

'I'm not here to put my pass in order. I'm here to see the social workers.'

'What is social worker?' he asked aggressively.

'They are on the third floor. They are the people who help cripples.'

'You mean the doctor?'

'No! The social workers.' Not knowing what social workers were caused him to let me go through. I was seven years old when they called me a headache, I suppose I just had to go on being one.

Inside was a hall with a giant horseshoe-shaped counter. Behind the counter were divided cubicles. In each cubicle sat a white clerk. On the hall side, opposite each cubicle, were bar-room stools where black interpreters sat. An iron grille divided the interpreters from the white clerks. Nowhere in this vast arena was there a place where the job-seekers could sit. This is where the queue ended.

The interpreter would hand your pass through the grille to the white clerk who would take his time studying it. If there was an irregularity, he'd give it back to the interpreter with instructions.

The interpreter would hang on to your pass which you didn't dare leave without. He'd then shout, 'Escort!' Two police would appear and escort you upstairs to the interrogation room.

If you fail to give satisfactory answers about why your work-seeking permits are not in order, they conclude that you don't want to work. You are then given twenty-four hours to get out of Johannesburg. Failing which, they charge you under Section 29. Two years' imprisonment. And after serving your sentence you still have to get out of Johannesburg.

If you tell them you were sick and couldn't come into town, they demand a doctor's certificate. Africans who have money go to private doctors and buy certificates. The best excuse is out. It doesn't work anymore because too many Africans have used it. It was to tell the authorities that you were mad in the township and that you were treated by a witch doctor. Witch doctors don't issue certificates.

The procedure is to give you a first job. If you find you don't agree with your employer because of the wage, or because the work is too strenuous or because your baas is just plain mean, as is often the case, they'll give you a second and third job. If you don't accept them, they declare you a vagrant by refusing to give you a fourth work-seeking permit.

The best thing to do is to take any work they give you and stick to it no matter what the circumstances are, while you keep your eyes open for a better job. You are bound to get it. The black man is not indispensable. We are a rotating labour force. Here, there are no middle-class Africans. Whether you're educated or not, you are looked upon as an illiterate and treated as such. In this building the worse sufferer is the educated African. If you've been a teacher you'll be offered a job as a grave-digger, or coal-heaver, or a domestic servant. They hate the sight of an educated African.

I know an African teacher who was married to a senior nurse. The nurse worked at Coronation Hospital. The teacher resigned from his teaching post because he flatly refused to parrot for the Government. He didn't believe in channelled 'Bantu' education. His beliefs lay in western education, not in 'Bush' education, as he put it. This teacher, or ex-teacher, found himself a clerical job with some private enterprise until he heard of a better-paying job in Germiston, some eleven miles out of Johannesburg. He used to travel in and out by train to his new place of employment. He had only worked there for about a month when he had an argument with the foreman, who fired him on the spot. Back to Influx he went with the view of finding another job, only to be told that he was no longer permitted to seek work in the urban district area of

Johannesburg. He was told to go back to Germiston.

When he pointed out to the authorities that his house was in Johannesburg, and that his wife was nursing in a local hospital, and also that he was born in Johannesburg, he was told that it was none of their business. They pointed out that he had violated the rules of Influx by having gone and worked outside Johannesburg, and that if he was found in the city, he was liable to be arrested.

Which he was. He was sold to a potato farmer. When he came back, he found that his wife had misbehaved. This was apparently too much for the ex-teacher. He cracked up.

I was limping up the stairs to the social worker's offices, when I heard the voice of an angry African shouting, 'Why do you tear up my J.C. certificate, baas?'

Then the voice of the black interpreter yelling, 'Escort!'

A social worker escorted me personally to numerous counters. After that, I was shown the way to the doctor. Before getting your first work-seeking permit, you are required to see the doctor. Not your own, but theirs, so as to be declared fit.

As I walked into the consulting room, I mean, hall, a degrading sight greeted me. Grandfathers, middle-aged men, teenage boys were made to stand naked in rows while a doctor gave their parts a sweeping glance. If he doesn't see a septic pimple on your penis you get a clean bill of health.

I could see old men hurriedly picking up their clothes from the floor and trying unsuccessfully to hide their nakedness by tying the sleeves of their shirts around their waists before putting on their trousers. They would then hurry out to get their work-seeking permits. Father was made to stand naked in the presence of son. The last layer of human dignity was being peeled off.

I made my way to the von Weilligh Street beer hall. It has since been removed. It was feared that we may one day run wild and harm the whites on our way home through the town.

As I turned left into von Weilligh Street, I nearly bumped into a well-dressed African woman who was having an argument with a European who was collecting money for charity. The African girl wanted to know whether she was collecting for black cripples or white cripples. I walked on.

As I came to the beer hall which was fifteen minutes walk from the Influx Control for a one-legged man and ten for a normal one,

I saw the queue. A black man's life is a life of queues, I thought.

I don't care much for this kind of legalised corn beer. I say legalised because we were not permitted to drink or make our own. We were only allowed to drink in municipal beer halls. What I don't like about this beer is that it takes a hell of a long time before it affects you. You've got to fill your stomach with the stuff first then do a lot of talking before you can get it going. There are times that I stop to wonder what makes us drunk – the noise in the beer hall, or the beer.

My reason for being here was to see if I could find some of the boys and be brought up to date with the latest local news. While I was working I hadn't paid them much attention. The beer hall used to be our regular meeting place.

At the time I was staying in a Hillbrow backyard with a girl who loved me strictly from a financial point of view. When she found out that I'd left my job, she would without hesitation replace me.

'Excuse me, my friend, could you please make a place for me?'

'Why should I make a place for you? I don't know you.'

'I've got one leg and I can't stand for a long time. This queue is too long.'

'I didn't make you one leg.'

'I know, I . . .'

'*Ag*, let him through, man.' The words came from a voice behind me. 'Can't you see he's sick?'

'All right, but these cripples worry me. They make the beer halls look unclean. Some crawl, some are . . .'

To hell with you, I thought, as I sneaked in front of him.

I stood inside the beer hall and looked at the familiar sight. To describe the noise is difficult, but if you've ever stood around a moody volcano you'll know what I mean.

Right there, at the entrance where I was standing, sat rows of dirty old men making business by straining the chaff from the beer with sieves. They charged a penny on a shilling mug.

The bastard in the queue outside was right when he said that the place was crawling with all sorts of cripples. They were everywhere, begging for a drink or for grains of tobacco. As for the mental cases, they could have filled a hospital.

It was a large cemented yard with rows and rows of long

benches. The benches were filled to capacity with corn beer drinkers. On these benches sat the Bandlas (fellow drinking members). There was no law that said you couldn't sit where you liked, but the code of the beer halls said that you couldn't occupy a place that belonged to a Bandla, unless you wanted to be bashed.

The dealer – he was the one who didn't have a shilling piece to contribute – was responsible for dishing out the beer. He'd fill up a shilling mug, the mug would be passed around and each member would take a deep drink before passing it on to the next.

This beer cannot be hurried. It's filling. If you drink it in a hurry, you take the gamble of vomiting. While it's being drunk, fights, domestic troubles, thefts, and life in general are discussed.

Picking their way carefully, so as not to spill or tramp on the drinkers, were the salesmen, the con men, selling cheap watches with expensive tags on them.

I stood wondering where the hell to look for my crowd in this ant-heap. There, beating on a drum was a mad man. He stopped beating the drum and started preaching. I moved nearer so as to hear. As I craned my neck, he moved away and started beating on the drum again. I kept on moving around.

'Duggie!' I spun around, nearly losing my balance. Sometimes I forget I've got one leg.

'Duggie! It's me, man!' It was Tiny. I hadn't laid eyes on him for months. He looked shabby, on the down and out. Life was making a mess of him.

'Come and join us, man. Where's your shilling card? You know you can't share or join our Bandla unless you have a shilling. Give me the card and I'll go and get your drink for you.'

I studied Tiny's friends and didn't like any of them. Maybe I had reformed.

'Where've you come from, man?' It was Tiny holding an overflowing mug. His fingers were dripping with kaffir beer. He wiped his brow with the crook of his arm without relinquishing the scale. 'I'm out at Orlando now,' he said. 'I'm boarding there. Hell, things are bad now, man, everything stinks, especially my pass. Nothing is like before.'

'Why don't you go and live in a hostel?'

'Shit, man, who wants to go and live in a compound with thirty other kaffirs? No privacy, no nothing. Gramophones, pressure stoves, concertinas, farting, vomiting and no women allowed. No, Duggie, that's not for me. I'm strictly a steak-and-egg man.'

Suddenly Tim, a trumpet player I knew, was beside us. In his hand was a sixpenny mug. That meant he was in a hurry, he wasn't going to sit with us long; otherwise he would have bought a shilling's worth. I made a place for him.

'How's the trumpet, Tim? When we going to start our band?'

'Haven't touched music for months, Duggie.'

'What's the matter? You're looking low, man.'

He took a deep drink from the mug. 'I've just been potato-farming.'

'How long?'

'Long enough.'

'Sorry. What's the story?'

'Usual. You know. I'm in bed, Sunday morning, reading the Sunday comics, when the cops come in. They want my pass. I shout to my wife to give it to them. She goes to the wardrobe, opens the proper drawer. No go. So she starts feeling all over her apron pockets. Still no go. I just lie there watching her. I can't move a muscle. She turns back to the wardrobe and starts flinging my clothes around. And she still doesn't find a damn thing. Now she's sweating, man! So she rolls me out of bed and starts flapping the blankets around. Not a sign!

'"Well," says the cop, "we haven't got all day."

'"Please, baas," I say, "she'll find it; she had it in her apron-pocket this morning."

'"Why does she have to carry your pass?"

'"I gave it to her yesterday when she went for permits to buy corn beer and to slaughter a sheep, baas. All our relations are coming, baas. We've just finished six months after her mother's death, baas."

'"*Lieg*," he shouts. "It's a lie! I can see you're one of those kaffirs who wants to make themselves Europeans! You sleep with pyjamas and read comics like a white man. Come along, your wife can bring your pass to the charge office. You say you've got one – I say you haven't!"

'Next thing, I'm standing in a line of handcuffs outside the police station. Then my wife's there, waving the pass book like a red flag. She gives it to the cop in charge. He looks at it, says it's in order . . . but it's too late! She must report with it to the Fordsburg police station next day.

'She starts screaming, at them, at me. "It was our baby!" she screams. "Our little baby boy! He was playing with it in the backyard!"

'The cop shouted, "March!" and I marched with the rest.

'Apparently, next day she was at Fordsburg with the pass book like the man said. But again, no go. I was gone, boy. Potato-farming. It took a lot of time, a lot of trouble, a lot of money to bring Daddy home again. And for now, Duggie, all I want to do is – nothing!'

As Tim picked up his mug to drink, I heard one of Tiny's friends say, 'Shezie here wanted to stab him. I said to Shezie, "Why stab him? Why kill the porridge and meat? Let's just take his money and clothes and let him go. This way we are keeping him alive for the next time. Killing him is like biting the hand that feeds you." Shezie here, he . . .'

I moved away. At the door I heard the voice of the mad man shouting above the din.

12

Walking, to a one-legged man, is like hard labour to a convict. That's what messed my pass up. The idea of walking to the Influx Control every day, just to be told that there was no work, became so tiresome that I stayed away.

I was sitting with my real leg resting on the bent knee of my artificial leg in a shebeen house, exhausted from begging the woman of the house to give me a scale on credit. Her refusal made sense. She wanted to know where was I going to get the money to pay her.

Right next to me sat a lone drinker. The man was mean, he wouldn't give me a drink. He kept taking a sip, then resting the scale on the floor between his legs.

'Pass!' It was the police, I didn't see them coming in because I was facing the wrong direction.

'You!' they said to the lone drinker. 'Where's your pass?' He gave it to them. After scrutinising it, they gave it back.

'What are you sitting so quietly for? Produce!' Reluctantly I took out my pass and gave it to him. He looked at it, then hung on to it. That told me that I was in trouble. One policeman was opening pots, and the door of the cold stove, while the other was peering under the unmade bed and up the chimney in search of skokiaan.

A voice behind me said, 'Hey, you, pick up that scale and let's go.' I looked at the man next to me, expecting him to pick up his scale, but the man sat tight.

'I'm speaking to you,' said the policeman, as he poked me in the ribs with a stick.

'Me?' I said truthfully, 'I haven't got any scale.'

'I say, pick up that scale and let's go!' continued the policeman aggressively.

I looked between the lone drinker's legs where his mug was kept. There was no scale. My eyes travelled slowly from his legs to mine, and there, next to my artificial leg, only half drunk, was the skokiaan scale. This wasn't magic; the bastard must have seen the police in the yard, before they came in, because he sat facing the window while I sat facing him, mutely begging him with my eyes to give me a sip. When he saw them, he must have pushed the scale right up to my artificial leg, I couldn't feel the scale touching me because the thing's got no life. I once did the same to someone. Maybe that's why I wasn't mad at the man. He gambled and won.

My man was sitting and facing me like I was facing this damn fool. (Funny calling a man a fool when he's just gone one up on you.) Anyway, I was chatting with the scale in my hands, taking my time, when through the little broken window I saw the yard crawling with police. I looked around the room where we were sitting, and saw that nobody else was aware of what I was aware of. I hurriedly took a deep drink then nonchalantly passed the scale on to the man next to me. He was just lifting the scale to his lips when a voice said, 'Hold it just where you've got it!' After giving me a dirty look, the man got up and departed with the police.

Now the same thing was happening to me. But I was not going to give in as easily as the man I had sent up. Not when I hadn't even got a drink from this man. Besides, the fine for skokiaan was five pounds or three months. If I went with them, it would be because my pass was out of order, not because of a skokiaan scale that didn't belong to me.

'Baas,' I said heavily, and with truth, 'this is not my scale.' But one look at him told me that no amount of pleading was going to change that wooden face. I looked around for the woman of the house but, as expected, she was nowhere to be seen. As for the man, he was already going through the door. The hopelessness of my situation made me pick up the scale. I prayed that we wouldn't tour the whole of Sophiatown before going to the police station.

Outside, I drew a sigh of relief, when I saw the men prisoners. It meant we were not going to roam much. Some of them had scales in their right hands, while the iron cuffs glittered on their left wrists. Most of them were just cuffed. That told me they were pass offenders. They didn't bother to cuff me, but I was told to walk right at the tail end so as to be under the direct eye of the police. At Anadale Street we halted, while another string of prisoners joined us.

All the time I had been praying for something like this to happen. If I had belched then, the stuff would have come back. Luckily, I didn't. I was having trouble with my eyes, I was trying to blink the tears back into my head. In all my life I'd never emptied a mug of skokiaan so fast. Now all that was left for me to do was to get rid of the scale. The bastard didn't even see me. It was too depressing to labour for something that didn't belong to me.

We were crossing the tram-line when I got rid of the empty mug. If it wasn't for the fact that they had my pass, which is something no man can do without, I would have tried to steal away at the first busy intersection. But without my pass, I was just as securely shackled as these prisoners.

After a louse-bitten night at Newlands Police Station, I appeared at the Fordsburg magistrate's court. It wasn't a question of guilty or not guilty, I was as guilty as hell. It was all there in the pass book, written in black and white. The only thing that they couldn't hang on me was the skokiaan, not when there was no exhibit. The magistrate must have taken pity on me, because

95

most of the offenders received six months to two years imprisonment. I got off with three months.

Again the gates of Number Four closed on me. But this time I was
a fourteen, not a long-time offender. Those sentenced from six
months to one year, were forced to have the one side of their heads
shaved clean, thus giving them a comical look. Black Red Indians.
Only those with long-term prison sentences were given the
privilege of having their heads shaved clean.

I was marched to cell number eight, known among the inmates
as the Prison Market. It's where the farm labour convicts are kept.
I was in cell number eight for three days before being auctioned
off. The farmer paid cheap for me because I had one leg. He
wanted someone who was disabled but who still had the use of his
arms to cook for his convicts.

The well-guarded lorry ride to Bethal somewhere in the Eastern Transvaal was uneventful. It was when we turned into a
muddy track that I became a little apprehensive. The track led to
some farm buildings.

I saw a large, rain-rusted zinc cottage and guessed it to be our
sleeping quarters. Hanging from paneless windows and blowing
gently in the breeze were potato sacks. To keep out the cold.

Sitting on the plank veranda of a large farmhouse was the
farmer. Four dogs were keeping him company. One look at those
saliva-dripping fangs told me that this farmer wasn't putting on
any floor show for our benefit. These dogs were real mean, and so
was their owner. These dogs reminded me of a picture I once saw:
Hound of the Baskervilles. One look at them and any idea of escape
became void. Something told me that they were not only vicious,
but that they were also well-trained.

A driver at the firm where I once worked told me that once he
was driving from Durban with the firm's car. When he came to a
village known as Howick he lost his way. Alongside the lonely
road, he spied a beautiful white-washed farmhouse with a long
drive-in road leading to it. After parking the car alongside the
road, he walked up the well-kept driveway, meaning to ask the
direction that would put him back on to the Durban-
Johannesburg highway. As he approached the house, he was
relieved to see the owner of the house sitting on the veranda,

newspaper in hand and sucking a pipe. Next to the master, and resting on its haunches, was one of these same vicious-looking dogs. Hat in hand, the driver approached the master, who he now saw was reading an Afrikaans newspaper. The newspaper supplied him with the clue on which language to use.

'*More, mynheer.*' (Morning, sir.) No reply. Only silence. Silence that made him feel he didn't exist. The master's eyes were glued to his paper. He cleared his throat and tried again, a little louder this time in case the master was a little deaf.

'*More, mynheer.*' Silence. The driver became uneasy. The atmosphere made him move. He took a step back. Then the hound growled, exposing merciless fangs. The driver stood pillar-stiff. The hound relaxed. The master kept on looking at his paper. Sweat streamed down the driver's face as he grinned vacantly at someone who wasn't even aware of him.

He wanted to transfer the weight of one foot to the other, when the hound growled again. He knew damn well the hopelessness of trying to run for it. He'd only be ravaged to death. Fear got the better of him, he started shaking visibly. 'Please, baas, *ek vra die regte pad*. Please, baas, I'm asking for the right road.'

Slowly the master looked up from his paper. The veins on his forehead were throbbing.

'Look,' he said in Afrikaans, as he pointed the stem of his pipe at the driver. 'In future, never refer to a white man as *mynheer*. To you a white man is a baas. Not *mynheer*. Understand? *Mynheer*, coming from a kaffir, means a kaffir preacher. You hear?'

'Yes, baas,' stammered the driver.

'Now, get your arse out of my sight.'

The driver went on to tell me that after the master had opened his mouth to speak to him, the dog didn't growl when he moved. When he neared the gate, he stole a look back. The man and his dog were sitting in the same position that he had found them earlier. That just goes to show how educated a country dog can be. As long as the owner doesn't open his mouth to you, you are regarded as an enemy. My new baas on the veranda wasn't saying a word.

As I prepared myself to get off the lorry in front of our sleeping quarters, I saw three labourers garbed in potato sacks. A hole was cut out at the sewn part of the sack for the head to go through, and two holes on the side for the arms. Uniforms, I thought. Another way of making escape impossible. Who wants to be seen wearing potato sacks in the streets?

The following morning we were all up at four a.m. I was warned to get up earlier so as to have breakfast ready for the convicts. Most of the convicts were made to dig for potatoes in the fields with their hands. Some were draining disused stagnant wells, while the rest cleared weeds.

It was difficult to keep count of how many we numbered because we all looked alike in these potato sacks. But there were three shacks like mine, and I was bedded down with about twenty prisoners. The only furniture in the shack was the potato sacks we used for blankets, and sleeping mats and the two improvised latrine buckets. These were emptied every morning by prisoners who were not strong enough to fight back.

The menu consisted of potato peels and thick porridge. Sundays, the diet was the same except for a piece of pork fat to remind you that it was a Sunday. Pork trotters would have been acceptable, but pork fat! As each week crawled by, I grew tired of it. When I get tired of a thing I get real tired of it. But just getting tired of it is not good enough. So I decided to do something about it. Life has proved to me time and again that a hungry stomach is a far better thinker than a skull full of brains. I started to plan, but I stopped planning, because to plan is merely an excuse to waste time.

The next day, I gonged the dinner gong. While the prisoners were busy looking as if they were enjoying the shit I cooked, I stole away to the nearby tool-shed where I busied myself with looking for the instrument that would serve my purpose. As luck sometimes favours the unlucky, I found what I was looking for. It was a piece of thick steel wire about twelve inches long. I filed both ends until they were dangerously sharp. Then I hid the weapon in the hollow of my artificial leg. We have a name for this kind of weapon, we refer to it as the 'chumenchu'. After you are stabbed with it, it leaves no visible marks; you bleed to death slowly from the inside; then Africans jump to the logical conclusion that you've been bewitched.

Me, I set out to bewitch all those lambs in that kraal and put the blame on snakes. The bastard would never find out as long as the

98

marks looked reasonably like snake-bite marks. One thing I was sure of: he wouldn't dare eat poisoned meat, nor would he risk the lives of his four pets.

Some people have patience; I have none. Not with the thought of roast lamb orbitting in the hollow of my stomach. I was softly whistling 'Chocholoza' as I made my way towards the sheep kraal. Christ! To think I used to live on cow's intestines twice a week, and maybe a quarter pound of beef on Sundays; yet here I was eating mutton left and right on a prison farm.

The only thing that the farmer said to me about his sheep that were dying systematically at the rate of one a week, was, 'You kaffirs are certainly courting death by eating meat poisoned through snake bite.'

'Baas,' I sighed, picking mutton from the crevices of my teeth, 'all I can say, baas, is that the devil looks after his own.'

Good things never last. I was beginning to look upon the farm as my home, when my three months came to an end.

13

As I jumped off the farmer's lorry at New Market, I felt heavy. As if my weight had increased. If it had, then it can be attributed to the mutton. Only my clothes gave me away. They were old and worn out. I resembled a real down-and-out crippled beggar.

Instead of going straight to my girl friend's place in Hillbrow, I went searching for a drink. When I finally did get to her place, it was late. I knocked, and a male voice told me gruffly to enter. Inside, I saw a burly, blue-black African sitting on the bed. The top half of his body was naked. And what a body! It was rippling with muscles. His bare feet were dangling inches from the floor. There was a long knife in his right hand. He was using it to clean the finger-nails on his left. The long nails were bluish with dirt. Not that I was thinking that that knife display was for my benefit. He didn't need it. Not with all those boulders and hills on his torso. Besides, I can tell if a man is trying to frighten me, and this one certainly wasn't.

Behind him lay my girl. The bitch was reading a newspaper wrong side up. She gave me one look, then completely ignored me.

'What for you want?' he growled. I made him north of the Limpopo because of his complexion and broken English. These Kalangas – that's the name we use when describing Rhodesians – brave the wilds of Bechuanaland and the Kalahari Desert to come to the Golden City in search of work, but mostly to get our light-complexioned girls. They have no family ties here; they are irresponsible, therefore dangerous. Imagine having to die at the hands of an illiterate.

When they get here, they find that they have walked right into road-blocks of language difficulties, because they know neither Zulu or Sotho, let alone English or Afrikaans. So the first thing they do is to lose themselves in white men's kitchens, as plain cooks or garden boys. This gives them four advantages: food, a place to sleep, a few shillings a month and the master's old clothes. They become domestic servants, something that we, the owners of Johannesburg, regard as work for females. We look down upon it.

Now the only way for Jackson here to get a light-complexioned girl, seeing that he can't speak her language nor she his (I might add that neither of them is prepared to learn the other's language—, is to buy her, i.e. give her money and buy her clothes. Something Sophie must have been praying for all her life, the bitch.

Have you ever tried taking a woman away from a man who has braved lion-infested country, and is at the same time faithfully bestowing her with the sweat of his brow each month? Try it. It's not listed on the Suicide Method List, only because the man who drew up the list hasn't come across this sure method of dying. I can assure you, brother, it's just as deadly as throwing yourself under the wheels of a fast-moving train.

'What for you want?' he growled again. I inspected the six-inch knife in his hand, then gulped. The bloody knife made me say,

'Doesn't Mary work here?'

'Who Mary?' he asked. I didn't know either. With the knife in his hand, I couldn't very well tell him that I was looking for Sophie, the bitch that was lying behind him.

'No Mary, baba.' The bastard was calling me *baba*, which means father, when he was far older than me. Mock politeness, I thought. Hopefully, I feigned dignity and slipped into the familiar bathroom where I spent the rest of the night.

I went back to the beer hall in the hope of meeting some of the boys. Perhaps they could put me up until something better showed itself.

I was in luck. Tiny. Still looking like the dark side of the moon. Still, the pot shouldn't call the kettle black; there I was looking like the letter W on a worn-out Welcome mat.

That night, after convincing his landlady that Rome wasn't built in a day, and that every dark cloud is lined with sixpences and tickeys, Tiny told me about Jeegar's death. Horrible as it was, this was one death I didn't mind hearing about. Jeegar was no favourite of mine. It's one of those take-it-or-leave-it stories again.

The thing that killed Jeegar was the promise of a life sentence. That's what a Judge promised him if he ever got himself into trouble again. The Judge's words were hardly cold when Jeegar found himself lying in hospital under heavy police guard. He was shot while trying to run away from a railway trailer. While in hospital he begged and cried for his friends to help him escape. If it wasn't that he had some goods hidden, I doubt if Tiny and the rest of them would have bothered about him. They decided to try after the bullet had been removed. Jeegar would still be under chloroform; that way, he wouldn't feel any pains while he was being carried.

That night, dressed as hospital orderlies, they managed to wheel him away under the noses of the two African police guards. They were just placing him in the car when they heard a police whistle. Their car shot forward, taking the turn at the hospital gate on two wheels. They gained speed with every lamp post they passed. Two cars gave chase. 'Make for Orlando Township,' Tiny said. He was sure that they could lose them there. It was easier thought than done.

Their driver did his best to lose the two cars. He turned into every street that they came to, but the two cars stayed behind as if they were being towed. At last their driver saw his chance and took it. There was a taxicab coming from the direction of Orlando Station. The driver pressed his foot down hard on the gas pedal, causing their car to shoot out like a police bullet. The tyres of the taxi screeched as its driver brought his foot down on the brakes. They missed a hell-bound train by a fraction of an inch. The car behind wasn't so lucky. It went bonnet-first into the taxi. Man, the crash was terrific!

They turned two blocks and were about to take the third, when their car stalled and the engine went dead. They tried to restart their car, but there wasn't a breath left in the engine. 'Let's carry Jeegar out of the car and try to lose ourselves,' someone suggested.

As they carried the limp form of Jeegar out of the car, they noticed that he was bleeding freely. The wound must have opened during the chase. They were trudging along a dark alley when they heard a police whistle for the second time that night. This time the sound came from the direction of the abandoned car. They got rid of the white orderly uniforms and lost precious time.

At the back of them, at no great distance, they saw the lights of torches coming directly towards them. Frantically they looked around and saw a field of long, dry mealie-stalks at the back of a house. You could just make out the house in complete darkness. Without hesitating they lifted the unconscious form of Jeegar over the fence. They were about to carry him deeper into the dry stalks when one of them slipped. With a thud, Jeegar fell face down. They heard a deep groan.

'Leave him!' Tiny whispered frantically. 'They can't see him. We'll come back for him later.'

In single file they made their way to the front of the house. When they came to the gate, they saw a number of people running up the street. They joined them. Everyone was running to the scene of the accident. From the crowd they learnt that the driver of the taxi was killed instantly, and the ambulance driver who gave chase was badly hurt.

Then a policeman elbowed his way through the crowd and whispered something to the sergeant. Tiny saw them moving away. They turned into the alley where Jeegar was stored. The one that led the way suddenly stopped and shone his torch on their white orderly garments. Then he saw the blood spots. With an oath, he followed them. They led him to Jeegar who was lying face-down in a pool of blood. He turned Jeegar's body and the first thing that the light showed was the horrible expression on Jeegar's face. The policeman gave three short blasts on his whistle and in no time the alley was filled with police and curious onlookers.

A doctor pushed his way through. He bent over Jeegar and then straightened up and said, 'He's dead. He died in agony.'

The police sergeant said, 'You mean the wound he was operated on opened up and he bled to death?'

The doctor wiped his forehead with a spotless white handkerchief and shook his head, 'See that corn-stub? Whoever was carrying him dropped him face-down, and by some freak chance the corn-stub stabbed him through the cut he was operated on. It went right through his gut. You can see the toe-marks of his bare feet – he was wriggling in agony! God!' the doctor said heatedly, 'this poor boy died horribly. I wouldn't wish the murderer of my own mother such a painful death!'

'God, Duggie,' shuddered Tiny. 'It was horrible. I mean the expression on Jeegar's face.'

'Still,' I said, 'his worries are over, and ours, at least mine, are just beginning.' If I had known just half of the truth of what I had just said, I would gladly have exchanged places with my left leg that lies buried somewhere in the Sahara Desert.

'What are your plans, Duggie?'

'At the moment, nothing.'

'It's a pity,' he said ponderingly. I looked up.

'What's a pity?' I asked suspiciously, without really wanting to know.

'It's a pity you've only got one leg.'

'What's my leg got to do with the pity?'

'I can't drive a car, and you can't drive a car, yet all we need is a car.'

'Leave the parables to Jesus Christ, Tiny, and tell me what's on your mind.'

'There's nothing on my mind, Duggie, except lots and lots of money, plus clothes to tide both of us over the winter. I know where, and I know how.'

'Tiny,' I said heavily, 'I was a transport driver in the army. I can do anything with any car, including locked ones. All I need is for you to press in the clutch if I tell you to.'

Tiny sat up with a jerk. 'No, man!'

'Yes, man!'

'Look, man . . .' He began to whisper furiously.

14

We were sitting in the stolen car. It was packed to capacity with stolen goods. Then we both heard it. The wail of a squad-car siren.

'Stop looking over your shoulder, and press in the clutch, damn you!'

'I'm not pressing in any clutch, I'm getting out of here!' I tried to grab him but he was gone.

The police found me sitting helplessly and resigned behind the wheel of the stolen car. . . .

When the dirty thought passed through my mind that I should mess up my pants so that the stench would make these prison warders leave me alone, I knew that I had just about reached the end of my endurance. The marathon beating-up had been going on for about three days. Again the thought passed through my mind, but I dismissed it. How can there be anything in your bowels when you've been three days without food? A baton hitting me on the side of the jaw rudely jarred such intentions from my mind.

Only half-conscious, I foolishly wondered what the hell two tasteless sweets were doing in my mouth. Then it hit me! These were not tasteless sweets, these were my front teeth. The bastards had knocked my teeth out.

'Are you going to use it now, kaffir?' The million-dollar question, I thought. I felt like screaming, but you can't scream through swollen lips.

'No!' I managed to croak the million-dollar answer. 'It's my property, not prison property.'

Again the baton flew. This time it landed on my ribs. Barely conscious, I heard the chief say, 'This is beyond me. I looked it up in all the prison rule books but I can't find anything that says that this convict is not right. After all, they did arrest him. And his artificial leg should be regarded as his property and not as part of himself. If he refuses to use it in prison, well, we'll just have to see where we can fit him. Maybe that's why he was sent to us. They didn't know what the hell to do with him at the Fort!'

'But,' said the warder exasperated, 'I can't have him hopping all over the damn place with one leg – besides, this bloody kaffir had his artificial leg on when he was arrested! Why shouldn't he use it in prison like he used it in that stolen car?'

'Wrong!' I thought. 'My artificial leg is innocent. It was Tiny's leg that was supposed to press in the clutch.'

'Don't forget,' said the chief, 'he also had his clothes on, a wrist-watch, a cigarette-case, a wallet, and small change that we are keeping as part of his property. Why shouldn't we keep his leg?'

'How in hell,' said the resourceful warder, as he pushed the peak of his cap to the crown of his head, 'is the bastard going to work if he's not prepared to use his artificial leg? I'm not running a jail for cripples!'

Nor did I ask to be arrested, I thought.

'You know the rules, Chief. They don't allow us to issue crutches as they may be used as dangerous weapons; now this black bastard has the gall to tell me that his artificial leg should be regarded as property and stored with the rest of his property. No, Chief!' pleaded Ambitious. 'Give me three more days and I'll make this kaffir wear his leg.'

For Glamorgan Prison, East London. My home for the next three years. Where I was drafted from Number Four. A prison within a prison. Home of the lost. Inmates have a name for it. They tag it the Shit House. The Afrikaners call it a *Straf Tronk*, jail of punishment. A prison where they confuse you for life in less than a year.

The warder got his wish. He dragged me to the segregated cells where the beating continued. He beat me in the morning before he started work, and in the evening when he was about to clock off. Hell, this man didn't even get a day off. He worked from Sunday to Sunday.

Whenever the door clinked shut on me, and I found myself alone, a depressed feeling clouded over me. I tried to laugh it off, as is my habit. Sometimes I would make jokes about my disability just to keep up my spirits, but the depressed feeling wouldn't go away. If I didn't have myself to blame, I would have cried. But I found it hard to pity myself because nobody was to blame but me.

Sometimes I felt like pacing the floor with my hands behind my back. But you don't pace the floor with one leg. You've got to hop, and hopping only jarred my brains. It also made me appear ridiculous. Imagine someone hopping up and down with his hands behind his back in the hope of trying to think out a solution. I had to try to preserve my energy. To try by all means to stay fit so as to be able to absorb the man's punishment. Because me, I'm not prepared to use my artificial leg in a prison. If it gets damaged, nobody is going to give me another one. I need it, it's my life. Without it, I might even sink lower in the outside world. Besides, it's too damn expensive.

The white man issues us blacks with wooden peg-legs. Only Europeans get legs that can be fitted with shoes. In fact, now that the war is over, they don't want to see a black ex-serviceman. They even go on to say that we blacks didn't fight, that all we did up north was to clean army boots. This makes me wonder whether it was a tin of shoe polish that fell on my leg, or a piece of shrapnel from Moaning Minnie's navel. So I was damned if I'd waste my leg in that rat-hole.

The following morning my cell door was rudely flung open. Instead of receiving my daily breakfast of moans and groans, I received a guest. A cell mate. He looked like an undernourished herd boy until you got to looking at his eyes. There and then I decided that this was no boy, nor had he ever been one. Not with those eyes. Milestones of hell. They were mud-red and deep-sunken. They told of a black past, a black present, and a blacker future.

One thing that stood out like the sharp points of a Zulu maiden's breasts was that this man-boy was ill. You could tell by the wheezing sound in his breathing, as if someone had punctured tiny holes in his lungs with a knitting kneedle, or as if he had swallowed a policeman's whistle. Brother, I thought, your days on earth are not as many as the fingers on your hands!

The Dutch bastard was bawling at the cell door. At first I thought he was talking to me, but what he was saying told me different. . . .

'You not only mucked your bloody cell with the shit from your bucket, you even plastered the walls with it, you dirty black swine! Sit on that bucket and empty your guts! The stomach-wash I gave you will produce those eight half-crowns you swallowed! When I come back in thirty minutes' time, I want to see that money lying at the bottom of that bucket – every penny of it!'

The cell-door clanked shut. The convict didn't even hear the guard. He was far too busy coughing his life away.

He was a shadow. You couldn't think of him as walking dead, because when you're dead and you walk, you walk because you don't want to stay dead. But when you're alive, and at the same time behave as if you're dead, then you have no respect for the living. When you added all this up, you got only one answer: waste. This man was nothing but a bloody waste.

At first I didn't understand what the prison warden was talking about, then I got it. The shadow had swallowed eight half-crowns. Now they were trying to get them out of him. The boys out at Number Four once spoke about stomach banks. This was it. To break the money-box, the prison guards give you a stomach wash with a syringe hose. Then they follow it up by forcing Epsom salts because the salts are as big as hail-stones. You are then placed on a toilet bucket and told to empty your bowels. Christ! I never thought I'd see the day they broke a stomach bank. Then something happened that very nearly made me scream foul! The shadow was playing foul. The bastard was re-swallowing the half-crowns as fast as they came out of his bowels. He wasn't even looking at them, let alone cleaning them. He gave me Zulu courage.

If this puny little man could openly defy his tormentors for so long – and it had been going on for days because I could hear them beating him up in the opposite cell – why should I give in to them so easily? They could go to hell and back and I still wouldn't use my leg!

And I did not. The morning after spending two days with my foul-smelling guest, I was made to hop to the prison yard where all the prison inmates gathered for their morning breakfast and daily orders. In this cemented yard that was surrounded by four formidable-looking walls, lay the heart of Fort Glamorgan. Whoever chose this particular spot for a prison must have had an intensive dislike for criminals. It is situated between the Buffalo River and the Indian Ocean. It's cold to freezing point throughout the year. There's a permanent visitor that frequents the prison every morning at six-thirty a.m. This visitor is so punctual that you could set your watch to it with dead certainty and never be wrong. Inmates have a name for this unwelcome visitor: The Mad Dog of the Ocean. Actually, it's a cold wind that blows from the sea. It has a mournful wailing sound like a dog that's being ill-treated by a cruel master.

When this mournful sound bounced off the four walls, it left us clouded in echoes of frozen misery. Our clean-shaven heads would be bleached with sea mist, our teeth would chatter, and our hands shake with uncontrollable spasms of hatred for this ill wind which has been responsible for many a convict's death.

One of the minor rules that added discomfort to misery at Fort Glamorgan was that when the convicts were gathered for their daily breakfast, which consisted of thick maize porridge, plus hot water dyed a dirty black and given the blessed name of coffee, it was an offence to sit flat on your buttocks. You were only allowed to rest on your haunches. Haunches! Hell, how can you sit on haunches with only one leg to support you! I sat flat! The convicts next to me giggled. After painfully forcing down the last lump of porridge that somehow got stuck in my throat, because coffee was only served to those who were serving sentences ranging from five years upwards, we were told to get up and line up.

Convicts working the East London harbour were first to be checked by the chief warden then marched out of the big gate escorted by six rifles and eight assegais. Then followed by the quarry span, then the plantation span, etc. At last my name was called. I was assigned to a platoon of twelve. Twelve bloody old men, I thought with disgust; these Dutch bastards have little respect for me.

As I understood it, we were to pick weeds out of the chief warden's garden. A nice and easy job. That is if you like picking weeds – God knows I don't. The only snag about this job was that the chief warden's house was situated on the other side of the prison, quite a distance from where we were.

'March!'

We marched. At least, I hopped. All went well as we passed through the big gate. It was only when we reached a newly-repaired gravel road that the soft sole of my one and only beautiful light-complexioned foot began to complain. From complaining it went to objecting. From objecting it started suffering. From there it was outright rebellion. I sat flat causing a minor disformation. In spite of the disruption, the platoon marched on. I thought I caught a gleam of amusement in the eyes of one of the old convicts. I couldn't care a damn. I was suffering, not him.

There I was, sitting flat on my buttocks in the middle of the road, busy massaging the sole of my foot. If they had given me one old shoe, all this wouldn't have happened. I might have made better progress. But now they know better. I suppose they do, otherwise I wouldn't have been there.

What was surprising was that my platoon guards hadn't missed me yet. Hell, I wasn't missing them either. But if those old convicts thought they could walk out on me, they had another thought coming. I looked around at my immediate surroundings, playing about with the idea of escape. Then I remembered that my leg was still locked up back there. Hastily I dismissed the idea.

Clever, I thought. Keeping my leg as security. They needn't have bothered, I'll never run out on any part of myself, not again. I've already left my real leg in the Sahara and I'm damned if I'm going to leave this one at Fort Glamorgan, whether it's real or not.

The thought of losing my artificial leg made me hop with renewed vigour after my platoon of convicts who now looked like the twelve disciples to me.

Ever tried hopping a long distance on one leg? Maybe you never had cause to. Well, I have. When you hop on one leg, you don't look where you're going. No. You watch the ground so as to see just where to place your foot on the next hop. This way you won't sprain an ankle. I was doing just that when I went charging after my squad.

When I looked up, it was too late. This was one collision that could not have been avoided. Not when I saw the guard's shiny boots right where I intended planting my next hop. I looked up too quickly, I shouldn't have. The back of my head got him squarely on the point of the jaw.

The contact was sickening. It jarred my brain, nearly causing me to black out. The only reason why I didn't lose consciousness, was the pain that seemed to spread like the tentacles of an octopus through my brain. An impact like two trains meeting headlong. I lost my balance and sat heavily on my buttocks, blinking the tears back into my eyes.

As for the prison guard, he was sitting directly opposite me. In fact, we were facing one another. The only difference was that his rifle was missing. Bashfully, I smiled at him, knowing quite well that what had happened was entirely his fault.

Then I noticed his glazed eyes. My God! The guard was out cold! I wanted to scream for a lawyer because I knew quite well what was going to happen to me.

Without a glance at me, the other guard went over to his unconscious companion and stood looking at him. After shaking his head once or twice, he sat on his haunches, it seemed to me, for a closer look. Then he pulled the skin under the glazed eyes of the guard. After that, he did a strange thing. He laughed. Christ, did he laugh! He laughed until he sat flat on his behind. I didn't like that. He was only going to make the unconscious guard more mad at me.

After what seemed an age, he got up, still laughing, and glared at me through tear-stained eyes. Then he looked about for his friend's rifle which he found lying four yards from where the incident had taken place. With the help of two black policemen, they got the injured man back on his feet. There he stood, swaying on rubbery legs, as if he had drunk skokiaan on an empty stomach.

Dazedly he looked for his rifle. His friend gave it to him. Then he squinted at me like someone who was looking directly at the sun. I just sat there waiting for them to help me up like they had helped him up.

'What do we do? Do we go on or do we go back?' It was the laughing hyena speaking.

'We go back, we'll never reach the chief's place with that thing along. I told the warder before we left the prison that I don't want that cripple convict in my squad. He told me that if we make this black bastard hop all the way to the chief's place, he might change his mind and use his leg. Cripples are bad luck; all cripples are bad luck, and as for this one, I'm going to make it my personal duty to escort him to hell and leave him there!'

In spite of the pain that was threatening to split my head into tiny atoms, I wanted to laugh at him. Because a missionary once said, all cripples are going to heaven, no matter what they do. He said it was better to enter the kingdom of heaven with one leg than with two.

'*Got!* I feel sick,' complained the guard. Who doesn't? I thought.

'When I reach the prison I'm going to book off and go home.' Good for you, I thought.

'About turn!'

'What about that convict?' asked the hyena.

'To hell with that convict!' came the fiery response.

When I saw that nobody was going to help me up, I got up painfully from the ground and started the painful hop back to prison. I was the last to go through the big gates. Everyone was waiting for me. Even the chief warden. This made me feel important.

For knocking the guard unconscious, and for refusing to use my artificial leg, I was placed in solitary confinement on half rations.

That didn't change me. I looked the same when I came out. I could have told them that I'd been living on half rations all my life. In fact, the advantage was mine because, through lack of sunshine, my complexion was lighter.

By now I should have been a hardened convict that nothing could move. But every time I thought of Majola, I became unhappy.

Majola was in the segregated cells with me. He was from the outskirts of Pietersburg, somewhere in the Northern Transvaal. He was sentenced in Pretoria and landed here at Fort Glamorgan, protesting his innocence every inch of the way. He was fifteen years old and sentenced to fifteen years' hard labour. Only his youth saved him from hanging. According to Majola's lamentations, and he lamented every minute of the five years that he'd been there, he wept for nothing else, thought of nothing else than his unfair arrest.

At first I didn't pay him much attention because there isn't a convict I know who's not suffering from unfair arrest. We are always innocent. Especially men like me who are found red-handed behind the wheel of a stolen car packed with stolen goods. Every Sunday after exercise they would bring Majola into my cell while the other convicts cleaned his. He had long ceased to use the sanitary bucket, and no amount of beating would induce him to.

Majola's diagnosis was simple. Majola was mad. But the authorities wouldn't believe this. They said he was shamming.

Majola's story went like this. He was a herd boy for some sheep farmer. Sheep are no good. They are stupid animals, quite capable of getting any man into trouble. The only good sheep is a dead sheep. I'm thinking of mutton.

One late afternoon while Majola was busy looking for a lost sheep, a storm broke loose that threatened to drown everything, himself included. Drenched to the skin, Majola vainly searched for shelter until finally, through sheets of rain, he saw a lonely hut. Relieved, he went to the hut and shouted a greeting from outside. A shrill voice from the inside said he could enter. Typical of all country huts, he had to go on all fours to get in. Inside, on a grass mat next to a roaring log fire, sat the oldest woman that Majola had ever laid eyes on. To him, this *go-go* (old woman) looked ageless.

After exchanging polite greetings with the ancient and explaining why he was there, Majola begged for shelter till after the storm. As he stood drying himself in front of the fire, steam emitted from his soaked clothes. The old lady said, 'Take all your clothes off, son, and hang them on the nail you see there. That way, they'll dry quicker.'

As Majola seemed to hesitate, she said, 'Don't mind nakedness in front of me, my child. I'm an old woman and only fit for the grave.'

There he stood, stark naked, enjoying the fire. He was oblivious of everything, especially the old lady. After all it was she who said that he shouldn't mind her. As the heat melted the cold in his bones, it also brought alive his sexual organ, but that didn't bother him, because he didn't feel any kind of urge. All the time the old lady was watching him covertly. She just couldn't pull her eyes away from the youthful figure of Majola. Maybe that's why her Adam's apple was bopping up and down in her wrinkled throat as she swallowed saliva after saliva.

'Son!' Majola stiffened, and the hair on the nape of his neck started to rise.

'Son, please, son, let me taste,' begged Eve in her last days.

'No! *Go-go*, no!'

'Just this one last favour, my boy, so that I can leave this world happily. Please, son, no one need know.'

After the act, the poor old darling sighed happily and died. It was as if she had waited for nothing else but that.

Fearful of what had happened, Majola dressed hurriedly in his clothes that were now dry. He was buttoning the front of his trousers when the old lady's great-grandson came crawling through the opening, dragging a bag of wood after him. One look at his grandmother whose private parts were still exposed, one look at the fear-stricken face of Majola, and he was convinced that his grandmother had been raped to death. In spite of the wrinkled smile on the dead old lady's face, they didn't believe Majola's story. He was dragged before a judge and charged with raping an old woman to death.

You might not believe Majola's side of the story, but I do. No one on earth would repeat the same story time after time for five years until he went mad and not be telling the truth. Anyway, Majola went to heaven to go and look for the old bitch with every intention of choking her to death. I know I would have done the same.

Majola died one morning. What remained of him was found in his cell. He bled to death after cutting chunks of meat from his own body with thick pieces of glass that he managed to break from his cell window.

★   ★   ★

Once again I found myself in the prison yard of Fort Glamorgan. Still without friends. Only with guards whose eyes glared naked hatred at me.

I didn't give a damn. I might have lost a lot of weight, but I certainly didn't lose my pride which was very important if you were going to be a successful cripple all your life. Besides, I'd won the Battle of the Leg. Because here I was assigned to the task of cleaning mugs in the prison-yard.

The prison was jinxed. I just couldn't seem to stay out of trouble. One night when all the prisoners were safely locked up for the night, I was somehow overlooked. I found myself sitting very lonely in the yard. You see, the prisoners' sleeping-quarters at Fort Glamorgan are located upstairs. Three storeys above the ground. The only buildings found on the ground floor, are the hospital, the kitchen, the prison offices and a special cell for the monitors.

If anybody thought I was going to risk my second leg by hopping up those steep-looking stairs, they had another thought coming. They could have gone right on thinking. I wasn't born yesterday. It might be better to have one leg, but it certainly isn't good to have no legs.

Though it shouldn't have been so frightening, it was. I mean to hear the same guard that I once had the fortune, I mean misfortune, to knock out cold, scream, 'Eeeeee!' in C sharp, when he saw me sitting on the bottom of the steps that led up to the prisoners' quarters.

He must have thought that he had locked up all the convicts for the night, yet there I was, sitting very lonely like the orphan I am. He sounded like someone who'd been knifed between the shoulder blades. Maybe he thought he was seeing a ghost.

'You!' he screamed, as if it wasn't me.

'Yes, baas,' I stammered. It was the first time I had addressed a prsion guard by the title of baas since I had entered the gates of Fort Glamorgan. I did it because I felt sorry for this boy who didn't know what to do with me. I think if I hadn't had less than a year to serve he would have resigned from his job. He clouted me with the bunch of cell-door keys on my clean-shaven head, leaving tiny dots of blood on my skull. Then he grabbed me by the scruff of the neck and started up the stairs at a running gait with me dragging behind in a sitting position. Each step hit me on the kidneys just above the buttocks. I was going to lose my manhood. I would never be able to produce children.

'You people don't seem to like me,' I moaned.

'That's a bloody understatement!' he said.

'Then why don't you let me go?' I asked hopefully. He was panting when we reached the door of my cell.

'Let you go? I'll see you in hell first, you one-legged bastard!' With that he banged the cell door in my face.

The next morning I was carried down the stairs by two convicts who accidently caused me to fall on my face as we reached the prison yard.

I was painfully picking myself up, when I felt, rather than saw, someone standing over me. Looking up, I saw the same guard of the night before. I braced myself for whatever was coming and groaned in advance. Instead of the expected rifle butt, I heard him saying, 'Report to the warden's office.' This man amused me when he talked, he couldn't pronounce the letter 'r'; he went *ghhhhh*.

When I entered the warden's office, the starch went out of my knee. It buckled, causing me to go down on all fours, I mean all threes. I had reason to. For sitting on a long bench directly facing me, were six of the biggest Afrikaners I had ever seen.

I wondered if they were real. When I last saw such big people it was out at the Church Square of Pretoria. They were standing around good old Paul Kruger, the father of Afrikaans history. Still, they were only statues. Now here I was seeing the same old bearded men. Only these were not statues, they were real flesh and blood.

Boers don't grow that big anymore. Sometimes I seriously wonder why. Now take these overgrown grown-ups of the ancient days, one look, and they reminded you of the playmates of 'Mad Dog' Chaka, bulldozer of Africa and Lion of the South. These were the originals. The true illegitimate children of Africa. Men who could haul a covered wagon from a muddy river without consulting any cows. Christ! I was due for some real trouble.

'Get up!' said the guard behind me. I stood up, holding on to the wall.

'This is the convict, *mynheer.*' They glared at me until I felt like a black piece of fat on the floorboards of a well-scrubbed cell.

One of them cleared his throat and it sounded like suppressed thunder.

'The members of the board of Fort Glamorgan have decided to set you free even if your sentence is not quite finished yet. We find that you are a worthless embarrassment to the authorities and a bad example to the convicts of this prison. It is felt that if you are kept here much longer, you will contaminate the convicts of Fort Glamorgan with your behaviour and give the prison a bad name.'

He looked around at the others, and they all nodded their heads in agreement. 'Dismiss!'

'Excuse me, sirs,' I said. 'This looks like an unconditional expulsion. If it is, how do I get home without a penny in my pocket or a jail warrant from you? You can't just put me out like that! Johannesburg is hundreds of miles away from here – besides, I didn't ask to be brought here.'

'That's your look-out.' The guard was dragging me away when somehow I got a few words across.

'When I get outside,' I shouted, 'I'm going to try and steal money for my train fare, and that might land me right back here!'

The words hit home. The results were instantaneous. The six giants turned blood red and the guard behind me gagged, I've never seen a rail warrant produced so fast. It was like magic.

When I got off the train at Johannesburg Station, it was raining in sheets. I stood undecided on the platform. I was wondering whether to take a bus to Sophiatown, or to squeeze my rail warrant to the end. Back at Fort Glamorgan I had made the authorities stretch it as far as Westbury Station just south of Johannesburg, near Newclare.

The crumpled piece of rail paper in the pocket of my old Army great coat decided me to go by rail. There was no point in wasting Government money. Besides, the station was right there. The bus-rank was some distance away.

I crossed the bridge and made for platform three and the Randfontein train. I hadn't been exposed to the rain yet, so I wasn't wet like most people around me. I was dry inside too. There was only one thought in my head, and that was for Sisinyana's skokiaan. It was as if I was possessed the way I was drooling at the mouth. Like a sex maniac in front of a nude statue. After forty-five minutes I dropped off from the Randfontein train at Westbury Station.

There's a big difference between Johannesburg Station and Westbury Station. Johannesburg is far too big, Westbury is far too small. But that's where the difference ends, because as far as the rain was concerned they are equal. It was raining just as hard here as it did back there. I pulled up the collar of my great-coat to shield my neck from the rain. I was about to walk through Newclare and get into Sophiatown from the direction of the second gate.

I passed through the station's entrance to begin the long walk. Nobody took any notice of anybody. The rain saw to that. When I asked somebody for the time, all I got was a look that said, 'Why don't you buy your own?' Instead of walking on the pavement under the shelter of the verandas, I chose the tar road because of its rough surface. I thought it better to suffer the onslaught of the downpour than to slip and fall on the smooth sheltered pavement. Past experience had taught me that an artificial leg doesn't agree with smooth wet pavements. The second reason why I was braving the storm rather than waiting it out under one of those shelters was because I was trying to get my clothes as wet as possible. If you think I was stupidly courting pneumonia, then I can tell you off-hand that were you in my shoes, you would have done the same! Have you ever had your clothes tied roughly in a bundle, dumped unceremoniously into a canvas bag and kept for three years in some hole they call a storeroom? That's what they did to mine at Fort Glamorgan.

I sighed with relief when I spotted the tram-line. It meant that I had less than a quarter of a mile to walk before reaching the big entrance that led to Sophiatown. I was walking with my head bent forward to keep the onslaught from getting me full in the face. When I reached the entrance of the second gate, I looked up.

Then I forgot everything. Past, present and future. Heavy raindrops lashed freely at my eyeballs, threatening to knock them out. I ignored them. You see I was staring. I didn't even blink. I closed my eyes tightly to drain the rainwater out of them. Also to make sure that the next time I opened them I'd see different. But it was not to be. I wasn't seeing things, I was seeing right. I blinked them again, then I started licking the rain from the tip of my nose and around my lips. The water tasted salty. I knew why. I was crying shamelessly.

Sophiatown was flat! A ghost town of grass and rubble. Slowly I crossed Main Road and stood stupidly at the spot where I had once waited for the baker's horsecart and helped myself to my daily bread. I looked up Good Street and could almost see the other end of it. Everywhere I looked, I saw nothing but grass and rubble.

I felt defeated. Like a king returned from war to find his kingdom smashed to dust. Worse even than that day in the tunnel when I came back home to find my father had sold the gramophone.

How I came to find myself at the corner of Victoria Avenue and Good Street, I'll never know. But there I was, standing forlornly at the deserted cross-roads of a black ghost town soaked in rain and despair. As I walked down Good Street, my artificial leg started to squeak. It was as if it felt the pain more than me.

Fort Glamorgan taught me one thing, and that was that crime was not for cripples. There was only one thing for me to do, and that was to look up Tim the trumpet player. First for a place to rest my head. . . .

Tim got me a job playing guitar for a jazz band known as the Black Crows. The Black Crows got me to Cape Town. No work, no food, too much booze put pay to the Black Crows, so I got me a job on a sugar boat as a potato peeler. This coaster did the runs between Durban and Cape Town, carrying cargoes of sugar.

When I got off at Durban, I liked what I saw. One look at the town and I decided that it was my kind of town. I was convinced that here a jazz band would prosper. Wrong again. . . .

15

'Let's try that number again.'

'Try it yourself. I'm so bloody hungry I couldn't blow my nose, let alone a trombone!'

'Look, Duggie, why don't you give it up? It's no use, man, we've been in this cursed town for more than six months now, and what's the score? V.D's got our vocalist for life and our buggered-up pass books are going to take care of the rest of us. These Zulus don't know a damn thing about jazz. They make me feel like going into the jungle to play for the monkeys! At least monkeys clap!'

'Fana, are you trying to start a mutiny?'

'Mutiny, shit! I'm just trying to get you to understand – remember your own words when you first recruited us at Johannesburg? You said that Durban was jazz-hungry. You said – oh, you bastard, you said – Durban's money bags were all tied up in melody, and all we had to do to untie the strings was drop a few blue notes. And look at us! Not only have we dropped blue notes, we've dropped every colour of the rainbow and still no damn money! You want us to keep on playing until we're blue in the face? To hell with you, man!'

'Wait, Fana.'

'What for? My pass is all crapped up because of that sweet tongue of yours.'

'Gentlemen, I think we should all get together and talk this situation over.'

'Situation, my arse! Look, Duggie, if you didn't have one leg, I would have beaten hell out of you. Why don't we just break up and let each one see his own way home? Why don't we, heh? Why don't we? Hell, man, that way we stand a better chance of reaching Joburg.'

'Fana, stop raving.'

'Better chance!' screamed a female voice very near hysterics. I turned; it was Zani, our vocalist. 'Duggie, don't listen to him! If we split, what's going to happen to me? Don't forget that it's through all of you that I've got syphilis. You practically pushed me into whoring with those foreign sailors just so you big brave men wouldn't die of malnutrition. Now that I'm practically rotting away, you talk about splitting up and deserting me! We . . .'

'You enjoyed every minute under those sailors!' interrupted Fana.

'Now . . .'

'Shut up! Fana, you want her to go on, and on, and on?'

'Yes,' continued Zani. 'As I was saying, we all came from Johannesburg together and we'll all go back together or else each one of you will see his mother!'

I left them to fling words at one another. This was our only daily bread. . . .

We were all sprawled on the floor, far too listless to get up, when in came Brother Joe. Joe was our bouncer and handyman. Just how handy he could be, you'll soon learn. I found him in Durban when he was on the down and out, having escaped some criminal charge up Joburg way. He came into the room that morning with his arms heavily laden with parcels. Sleepily I watched him as he unloaded the parcels on the unsteady little table. As each parcel was being unloaded, my eyes grew wider.

I nudged Fana, who lifted his head and looked. Fana turned right round and resumed his interrupted sleep. He must have thought that he was dreaming, because I heard him whimper. Then he suddenly jerked, knuckling sleep out of his eyes so as to see better. He shook me roughly without shifting his eyes from the little table, as if afraid that what he saw might disappear. Well, it did not. It was food, and it was real. Six loaves of Jewish bread, six bottles of fermented milk and four tins of beef. After the feast everyone blessed Brother Joe.

As usual we had all prepared to go our different ways. There were no rehearsals. I was getting into my jacket when I heard Fana asking nobody in particular if they hadn't seen his shoes. No one seemed to be taking any notice of him. Then Fana turned to me with the same question. I shook my head. The formidable-looking form of Brother Joe was fast asleep in the corner, both his hands resting on his protruding stomach.

'Try Brother Joe,' I suggested. Fana went to Brother Joe. Usually it was dangerous to rouse Brother Joe when he slept, but this was an emergency.

After carefully waking Brother Joe, Fana said 'Brother Joe, I'm sorry, but have you seen my shoes?' Joe blinked, then yawned. Fana repeated the question.

Then Joe nodded. 'I sold your shoes this morning and bought food with the money.'

When Fana continued staring stupidly at Brother Joe, his mouth hanging open, Joe hastened to add, 'I didn't hold anything – honest, Fana. If you won't believe me, I can take you to the rickshaw shed where I sold them.'

First, Fana looked like he was going to vomit. Instead he sat down heavily and cried. Brother Joe looked at him, shook his head, turned over and started snoring. It's not pretty to see a middle-aged man crying. There's something awful and sickening about it, especially if he's bearded.

'You – you – you sold my shoes, Brother Joe? Why, man, why?'

Without turning his head, Brother Joe said, 'Number one, I didn't want you to die of hunger. Number two, I could have done it to any of you, only your shoes happened to have been the best.' Fana went out into the back yard, his tears rolling into his beard. From then on, it was dog eat dog. Every man slept with his belongings clutched tightly to his bosom.

When we first came to the cottage at Victor Lane some seven months before, the Indian landlord had agreed to let it to us for seven pounds a month. We paid for the first month all right. The second month, our shows went bad. We suffered a string of flops. Most times there wasn't even enough money to pay for the hall after the show.

Secretly, without the knowledge of the landlord, we hired out one of the rooms to a Zulu washerwoman. Whenever our pangs of hunger reached an unbearable peak, we would force this woman to pay her rent in advance, or threaten her with eviction even if she had paid only a week before. We would point out to her the importance of paying the rent in advance. Now she was a year ahead in her rent, so that dried up our only source of income.

You could ask why we didn't look for work. Work was out of the question. In the first place, we were looked upon by the authorities as illegal immigrants. If the Durban police found out that we were citizens of Johannesburg and not of Durban we were sure to be arrested, even if Johannesburg was only four hundred miles away. Our pass books carried the Johannesburg stamp, not the Durban one.

The more I thought of our situation, the more hopeless it seemed. Christ! It was as if we were marooned on another planet with only one wish: to come back to earth – I mean Johannesburg.

Listlessly, I opened the door to one of the bare rooms and there was Timothy's lean black body. Tim, our first trumpeter – you could actually count his ribs. He was trying to keep his balance with one foot while he pushed the other into the sleeve of an old, worn-out, navy-blue jersey. He lost his balance and his bony buttocks collapsed on the floorboards. Sweat streamed down his face.

He was so intent on what he was doing that he wasn't even aware of me. It was only when I coughed and said, 'Tim, if you want to make that jersey underpants, why don't you cut the sleeves a little bit higher to make allowance for your thighs? Or aren't your thighs bigger than the top half of your arms?'

He looked searchingly at me as if trying to determine whether I was mocking. After satisfying himself that I was quite serious, he said, 'They are my last damn trousers! The seat is so full of patches that I'm damned if I know where to put the next one.' Broodingly he added, 'It's a sin for a man with no wife and no children to wear trousers like these.'

'We were talking about the jersey, not the trousers,' I reminded him helpfully.

'Yes, yes, the jersey.' He sighed, looking down at his knee where the sleeve of the jersey was stuck. 'All the same, it's through the trousers that the jersey is suffering.'

I didn't get it. As far as I was concerned, Tim was the only one who was in trouble and suffering. Still, I allowed myself to ask,

'What do you mean, "it's through the trousers that the jersey is suffering"?'

'The way you play your guitar, Duggie, convinces me that all your brains are in your fingertips. There's nothing up here,' he said, pointing with the scissors at my head. 'Look,' he said, with patience that I never dreamed he possessed, 'we agree that the seat of my pants has so many patches that it looks like a cabbage, right?'

I nodded my head, and with the corner of my eye searching for a place where I could sit. I was getting tired of standing.

Diplomatically, he said, 'If we want to camouflage the hole that's going to get me arrested for indecent exposure, without adding another patch to the batch of patches, what do we do?'

'I don't know. You see, my trousers haven't got a hole.'

'I know, damn you! I wasn't talking about your trousers, I was talking about mine. Who wants to hear about your bloody trousers?'

'Sorry.'

'Well,' he said, 'where was I?'

'You said something about your buttocks getting you into prison.'

'Not my buttocks, man! I was trying to teach you what to do if you ever found yourself in such a predicament.'

'What the hell you making a cross for?'

'Nothing,' I assured him. He scowled.

Pointing at the jersey, he explained, 'I was going to camouflage my buttocks – I mean, the hole in my trousers, by putting a patch directly on my buttocks – I mean, by wearing this jersey as underpants. But now,' he looked morosely at the jersey, 'the damn sleeves are too small for my thighs.'

'Look,' I said, as an idea hit me, 'why don't you tie the sleeves around your waist with a pin and let the bottom half of the jersey hang over your behind, and then wear the trousers on top?'

He brightened up. 'Maybe I made a mistake about your brains being in your fingertips.'

'Yes,' I said, and there was a sarcasm in my voice. 'My brains only come to my fingertips when I play the guitar. Most times you'll find them in my head.' Then suddenly I laughed. I laughed until tears streamed down my face. Tim looked at me, then

123

slowly nodded his head. Something like this had to happen after the way we'd been living these past few months.

'Don't worry, Dug,' he said. 'I assure you I'll stick with you. I promise I won't desert you – just as long as you don't become violent.'

'What the hell are you talking about?' I asked wide-eyed.

'I thought your brains were going the way of your leg.'

'Nonsense, Tim. You know what I was laughing about?' He shook his head. 'Cape Town. The Black Crows in Cape Town.'

He didn't look any the wiser. How to explain?

Durban is only four hundred miles away from Joburg, and if we had the strength and clean passes we could have walked it in less than a week. But Cape Town is nearly a thousand miles away from Joburg. You travel on that train until you come to think that the driver is either going in circles or that he's on the wrong track. In Cape Town The Black Crows had it bad – we ended up without musical instruments. Without anything. But what had really made me laugh was remembering our second trumpeter. He was a lot like Tim.

I once found him sitting quietly on the doorstep of a house in District Six. He looked so troubled that I found my heart going out to him and I went up to find out what was eating him. He just stared and stared, ignoring me.

After a time, he said, 'Duggie, my shoes are so worn-out that it's just through habit that I put them on every morning. I'm telling you, Duggie, I walk alongside them and both the shoes and myself know it. Yet our pride won't let us part, or admit the fact. Only common decency keeps us together. My shoes are dead, Duggie, but it's hard, my friend, very hard to part with something that has walked the lonesome road with you without a single complaint. As I say, Duggie, my shoes are late but we won't admit it. But that's not my real worry. I only notice them when I happen to look down; and that's not often, because I don't have to look at what I don't want to see. The thing that's giving me real hell, the things that're threatening to drive me out of my senses are really my trousers.'

I must have looked confused, because he continued, 'If your trousers are torn at the back, Duggie, it doesn't matter so much because you can't see it except maybe when the wind blows in and you feel a draught. But when your trousers are torn at the knees, Duggie, it's pure hell, brother. Every time you sit, the very first thing you see are your dirty knees. They don't only remind you that your trousers are torn, but that you need a bath badly, too.'

Cape Town. I hated the bloody town and all the people in it. The coloureds for instance.

You know what my introduction to Cape Town was? I had got off the train at Cape Town Station and started looking around for the toilet. I found it next to the station's entrance. I passed through the door marked 'Non-Europeans'. Inside, I was confronted by four closed doors; written on each of these four doors were the words: 'Insert Penny to Turn Slot.' You have to pay to relieve yourself.

Standing in front of one of these closed doors and discussing women were two rough-looking Coloured characters. Just as I approached the first door, it opened and someone came out. Without breaking my stride I went in and closed the door behind me.

Man! I never heard so much abuse thrown at me in all my life! These characters have got no pennies of their own, so they wait for someone to come and use the toilets and when he comes out they block the door before it locks itself. This way, they get a free shit. I've never in all my born days heard such swear words. They started with my great-grandmother and ended up in the maternity home where my mother was the leading lady. Then one of them suggested that I should be shaved. That meant they were going to go over me with cut-throat blades. Hell, there was only one thing to do, and I did it. I took a handful of loose change from my pocket and sprayed the coins over the top of the door . While the swines scrambled for the money, I opened the door and sneaked out. But not before I heard one of them say, 'You're lucky, kaffir Yank.' That's the name they use for blacks who are smartly dressed.

But that's not the real reason why I want nothing to do with the Coloured race. The real reason started just when I crossed the parade grounds into District Six, the Coloured man's domain. I was suffering from a hangover that nothing short of foaming skokiaan could fix. It was threatening to drive me dog-mad. After

125

racking my brains for a substitute, I decided on brandy. But the trouble was, we blacks weren't permitted to enter liquor stores, so I was forced to look for a shebeen.

Just off Castle Bridge I saw a Coloured man who looked like he could help me out. After chatting a bit, I asked him if he knew of a place where I could buy some brandy. He thought a while, and then he said, 'I know a friend who knows of a place where you can get fixed up.' He led the way and I followed happily.

In a few minutes we were at his friend's place. His friend said after we told him what we were looking for, 'That's easy. Come along– I know of a friend who knows a friend that knows the spot.' I should've smelt a rat then, but I didn't.

When we reached the friend that knew a friend who knew the spot, that friend said, 'You shouldn't have gone to all this trouble.' Subconsciously I agreed with him. Because, he went on, his friend's friend knew of a friend that actually has a friend whose only friend owned the best shebeen. . . .

I ended up entertaining more than a dozen Coloured bastards. When I finally joined the rest of our band members, I had a lousy two-shilling piece to my name out of three whole bloody pounds!

Do you want the Coloured in a nutshell?

When God said to the Afrikaner, 'What is your major wish?' the Afrikaner answered, 'All I want, Lord, is strength and fertile soil.' The Englishman, when God asked him, replied, 'Education, Lord, education!' When He turned to the Jew, the Jew tapped his head and said, 'Brains.' Before God could say another word, the black man said, 'I'm a simple man, Lord. All I want is a pick and a shovel.' Then God turned to the Coloured man and said, 'Well, what can I do for you, my good man?' His hands in his pockets, the Coloured man turned and looked at the black man. He shrugged his shoulders and said, 'I was just keeping him company, Lord. . . .'

To get back to Durban. . . . At last, one morning, I was able to call a meeting. Thomas was the last to come in.

'Is everyone here?' I asked.

Thomas nodded. 'Except Alpheus. It's his turn to do guard duty.'

'Never mind, get him. I'm beginning to think that it's necessary. That Indian landlord was just bragging when he said he was going for the cops.'

'Where's Zeblon?'

'He's scared to put his foot in here since he pinched the washerwoman's boss's shirt from the washing line.'

'How does she know he pinched it?'

'How couldn't she, when that's about all he's wearing?'

'All right, all right. Just get the rest of them in here. This is important.'

'Early this morning,' I told them, 'I spoke to an Indian by the name of Hadjee. He owns a café-night club. Hadjee has agreed to sign us on for Saturday night on a fifty-fifty basis. We don't pay for the use of the club and he doesn't pay us a fee. Whatever money we make, we split fifty-fifty with him. I also checked on the ships. There'll be at least four American cargo-ships in the harbour on Saturday night. So no matter which way the dice roll, we must come out with something.'

Sunday morning, as we came back from Hadjee's night-spot, everyone was in high spirits. Even Zani had forgotten the sores on her feet. The show had been a near-success. I was the only one who felt depressed.

They all gathered in the room. 'I'm happy to tell you that we've scored exactly ten guineas. Enough to get five of you to Johannesburg.' They all beamed. The bastards. Not one of them was interested in knowing what was going to happen to me. To hell with them, I thought. The sooner they get out of my sight, the better.

After giving each his two pounds one and six, which was a single third-class fare to Johannesburg, I was left with a half-crown.

'Now, Fana, Tim, all of you. Before we part I'd like to thank you for sticking with me so long.

'In Joburg you are going to have a lot of trouble straightening out your passes. You haven't renewed your work-seeking permits. If you say you were sick, they'll ask for a doctor's certificate. To go to a private doctor for one is asking for trouble; they know that private doctors can be bought.

'So your best bet is this: go to the address on this piece of paper. You'll meet a friend of mine there. He goes under the name of

Zuluboy. Zuluboy will put you in contact with someone who will get you prisoners' discharge papers. They'll be quite genuine; it will be written on them that you have been released from Leeukop prison – that's where they keep the vagrants. Those papers are the only ones that will save you from a six- to nine-month prison sentence. Don't be ashamed of carrying such papers. In this country it's not a disgrace for a black man to have been to prison; prison to us is just a break from monotony. So if such papers can be of some use, why not make use of them? Me, I know of no other way, and I should know.

'Another thing, go to Singh's Billiard Saloon. There you'll find Hakkeltjie, the Coloured drug smuggler from Cape Town. Ask him to go and buy your rail tickets for you. We blacks can't buy long-distance train tickets without the proper travel documents.'

When everyone had gone, I looked around the bare room and felt a lump in my throat. Legal or illegal, everything I touched turned black.

I took my last crumpled cigarette from my pocket and made myself comfortable in one of the corners of the bare room, to wait for darkness. I didn't dare venture out this early. Not while I owed all the shops in Grey Street food money.

One thing was certain, I'd have to change my sleeping quarters. But where to go to? Durban stank of one problem. All the domestic servants were men. In Johannesburg we have women. You could always make love to one of them and live with her in her room at the back of the master's house. No rent, free food and one or two of the boss's shirts while he imagined that they were in the wash.

In Durban there was no such thing. Otherwise I wouldn't have bothered with sleeping accommodation. I would have done what I used to do back in Johannesburg: made love to one of the working girls and lived with her, even if living in the back yards of white men's houses is not without its ups and downs.

I'm reminded of one night when I went to my girl's room at the back of a white man's house. It was late when I got there and my girl must have long been through with her duties. What I really remember about that night, is that it was so cold that my nose wouldn't stop running. When I got to the room I knocked. But there was no reply. I tried again, still with no results. I made for the spot where she always kept the key for me to find when she was on her day off, but I drew blank.

Again I repeated the knock and still nothing happened. I was afraid to knock loud for fear of waking up the house. That time of night they have a dangerous tendency of shooting first and asking questions after. After repeated knocks, I gave up. I decided to think.

One thing stood out like the point of a Zulu warrior's spear, and that was that if I tried reaching Sophiatown at that time of night, I would end up in jail for not having a night special.

I looked around for a place to spend the night, but could see none. Then I realised that I was leaning against one of those giant trees that are so frequently found in white gardens. Without a moment's hesitation, I climbed the tree, meaning to spend the remainder of the night there. Better a human bird than a jail bird.

I must have dozed off because something startled me. I would have fallen head first to the ground if I hadn't taken the precaution of tying my belt to a branch and then around my arm. I peered into the night hoping to see what it was. Then I heard a noise coming from my girl's room. Someone unfamiliar with the mechanism of the lock was fumbling with it from the inside.

Hurriedly I undid my belt from the branch. My fingers were numb with cold and my descent was not without hazards. Finally, I made the ground with little more damage than bruised hands and a tear in my pants. I was in time to see a stark naked figure emerging from the door and making his way to the toilet which was situated on the other side of the garden. Like lightning I went into the dark room and locked the door behind me. I groped towards the bed where the bitch was deep in sleep. Undressing quickly, I crawled into bed. As my icy body came into contact with hers, she moaned and said, 'Why so cold, dear?'

'Shut up, you bitch.' I felt her shiver, and knew it was not from cold.

I waited. Then it came. First softly, then loud, then louder, then frantic. It was the naked bum outside. Unlike him, I raised my voice triumphantly and said, 'Climb the tree, pal, climb the tree.' As usual, I'm not the brainiest of men. There are people with far more. This son of a bitch pushed the mouth of the garden-hose through the small window, and before I knew what was happening, the water tap was turned on full force, soaking me, bitch, blankets and all.

I checked to look at the time on my wrist, then remembered that my watch was in the pawn shop. It was dark outside, time for me to get going, I groped for my walking-stick, then decided to stick around a little longer. Think before you move. Having reviewed the wealth of accommodation alternatives, I turned my attention to thoughts of transport. Four hundred miles, more or less. Do I walk it? Thanks. Stow away on a train, ride in the toilet? My jaw itched, thinking of the sturdy fist of the law. Which left me with one alternative. The one I hit Durban in when I came down starry-eyed to book halls and accommodation for my players. I call it my Jonah trip. You know the Bible story of Jonah and the whale? That's the story, except Jonah began in a ship. I began in the whale.

At eleven o'clock every Saturday night there is a special closed news van that leaves Johannesburg to deliver the Sunday newspapers to Durban. This van arrives here in Durban about two hours after midday.

That knight at Marshall Street I was drunk. I watched them feeding the red monster with endless bundles of newspapers. There was a Zulu man who worked inside the mechanical whale. Every time a bundle was heaved into the van, he would drag it further in and pack it. When the van was finally loaded, I walked unsteadily nearer so as not to be left behind. The driver was about to close the doors when he chanced to look over his shoulder. 'Get in, get in,' he said. I nearly asked, 'In where?' because I could see no place to perch myself. But that would have been looking a gift whale in the mouth.

I found myself lying flat on my back, both arms pressed tightly to my sides. The tip of my nose was two inches from the roof of the van. The driver slammed and locked the doors, shutting out the only light that came from the street, leaving the insides of the van in complete darkness.

Man, sardines were a hundred per cent better off. The damn things were at least dead. The four-wheel monster started to move. At the same time my misery which was hitherto only misery, became painful misery with every turn. The knob of my walking stick, which was pressed close to my side, seemed about to cave my ribs in. If my presence wasn't illegal, I would have taken the matter up with the news manager. Then I made a hair-raising mistake, I dozed off. When I came to, I nearly screamed. You see, I had forgotten where I was. As I tried lifting myself, my head banged against the ceiling, leaving a lump as big as a dove's egg on my forehead. I tried lifting my knee but only succeeded in banging it. As for the top half of my body, it wouldn't move at all. This brought me to the logical conclusion that I was in a nailed coffin.

I was about to fill my lungs with whatever air there was and scream like hell, when I heard a baritone voice praying in the Zulu language. I was damn sure it was my ancestors, though I didn't think I wanted to meet them. Not if they were going to inquire about my past. Imagine my relief, when my drink-befuddled brain slowly recalled the incidents of the past few hours. As for the voice that seemed to come from the long departed, it really belonged to that African worker who had been packing the bundles into the back of the van. To ease my fear, I began a shouting conversation with him.

He told me that in spite of the fact that he was on this run for three months now, he was damned if he could get used to these trips. Just the idea of being locked up in a closed van with only one door that couldn't be reached in an emergency because of the bundles of newspapers, and even if you could reach the door wouldn't open because the lock was on the outside, was enough to make any man cling to God's apron. I didn't blame him for drowning his fear in prayer. I know I would have done worse.

That was how I came to Durban, and that was how I was going to have to go back. But this time, I wouldn't have to worry, because, when the van goes back, it goes back empty. No newspapers, no inconvenience. . . .

16

A knock sounded through the whole house. Police, I thought; never underestimate an Indian landlord. The door was flung open and someone was shouting my name. It was Tim. I'd know that voice anywhere.

'What's up?' I called.

He was out of breath as he said: 'You remember you told us to go to Hakkeltjie for our tickets?'

'Yes,' I said.

'Well, Hakkeltjie took the money, all right, only he bought his own ticket to Cape Town. He's gone, I tell you, gone! Gone! Gone!'

I groaned. I had forgotten Hakkeltjie's soul-dream. In fact it was no different from ours. He was forever dreaming of the day when he would return to his happy hunting grounds armed with a bottle of red wine in his back pocket.

'You tell me how the Coloureds make out by living off the next man, yet you still send us to them. If I didn't see him jump on the Cape Town train with my own eyes, I would have said that you're in with him. What I want to know from you here and now is how the hell are you going to get us out of here? What are we going to do?'

'Wait, Tim. Let me think.'

'Don't!' he almost screamed. 'I don't trust your thoughts – just get us out of here!'

'I know how to get myself out of this mess, but definitely not all of you.'

'Why not all of us?'

'Because that Dutch driver will never agree to a mass removal – it might get him into trouble.'

'What driver? What the hell are you talking about?'

'Hang on,' I repeated, 'let me think.'

'But I don't trust your thoughts. . . .' Tim began again.

I was tired of hearing these words, so to shut him up I said, 'There's only one thing we could do, Tim.' His eyes brightened up. I could actually see the whites of his eyeballs in the gloomy room.

'What, Duggie, huh?'

I let him stew a bit before saying, 'We could sell your trumpet.'

'Sell my trumpet? Are you mad?' He was shaking visibly. Sometimes I had wondered who came first, himself or his trumpet. Now I knew.

'Where the hell will I get another outlet for my misery? Tell me, man, tell me that!'

'You can always buy another,' I said slowly, hedging away.

'This trumpet to me, Duggie, is like that artificial leg is to you. Inseparatable, inseparatable, see? So see that you keep your dirty mind out of it.'

'All right, Tim, I was only pulling your leg.'

'Pull something else, you bastard. And,' he added meaningly, 'if anything should happen to my trumpet, I'll know who's responsible!'

I cursed myself. Now I was stuck with the job of seeing that nothing did happen to his bloody trumpet. This task would have been easy if Brother Joe wasn't living amongst us.

'All right, all right, damn you, forget it! Where's the rest of the gang?'

'Zani went wild, she dashed off shouting for the police at the top of her voice.'

'Hey, she could get us all into trouble!'

'No, we caught her. She led us one hell of a chase, but we managed to bag her just off Smith Street.'

'Where are they now?'

'At the Esplanade. Fana is trying to talk some sense into her. She'll be O.K.'

Poor Zani, I thought. That running must have opened the sores on her feet.

I could understand Tim's horror at having to part with his instrument. In Johannesburg, whether you're working or not, it's hard to have ten whole pounds all at one time. As for twenty-five, the approximate price of Tim's trumpet, well, that's completely out of the question. If you buy it on the Play-

While-You-Pay scheme you are sure to be the loser in the end.

In fact, many things can happen to you before you come to the last instalment. You'll find most of them listed in your pass book which more or less tells you not to get sick, see that your rent is paid on time, plus your tax, be out of any white area by ten p.m., do not choose work, just take work, because as I told you before, you are only allowed three work-seeking permits and when you go for the fourth, they hang a vagrant sign on you, then send you to the nearest potato farm. When you come back, they endorse you out of town. How the hell can you finish instalments with odds like that stacked against you?

Tim certainly wasn't exaggerating when he spoke of his trumpet as the only outlet to his misery. He was not going to be long for this world. He put too much emotion in his playing, tugging and tugging at God's apron strings like a jealous disciple that wants to be noticed. I sat in the yard with Zani and the old washerwoman. His sound came through the back door. A mournful, bleeding sound.

Jesus! The old washerwoman – it was as if she was in a trance of some sort. She was rocking from side to side in time to the wailing of Tim's trumpet. The balls of her eyes were protruding. She was not of this world. Even poor tired Zani with her raw painful feet was fascinated.

Suddenly, the music broke off. There was a slight commotion. I got up to go and find out why Tim had so suddenly shut off his sweet, haunting music. As I sidestepped the old lady at the door step, she said, 'You know why I don't mind so much when you boys crook me out of my money?' Before I could frame an indignant reply, she said, 'It's because of the beautiful music that that boy makes.'

Inside, I found Joe. He was with three American merchant seamen. They were in search of drinks and girls. This was good. It meant we were going to eat. After that, anything might follow. Negro seamen are noted for their generosity. We could expect anything.

Something did follow. We got money for food, plus a promise of some second-hand clothing. When their ship sailed for some distant port, blues settled on us again.

Without a moment's hesitation we agreed that Joe should take and sell the second-hand clothing at the rickshaw sheds where they buy and sell anything, including fat from a white woman's rump. They claim this fat, if rubbed on the right spot, could secure you the post of boss boy in any firm. Or if you want the dirt from a monkey's toenail, to stop a leaking ear, that's the place to get it.

They even sell gent's socks. You can get new ones, second-hand ones, dirty socks – you've got to wash these yourself. Then there are the darned socks. The ones with holes in them are the cheapest.

While Joe was gone, I tried to think of a way to get the gang out of town. I was becoming desperate. I thought of selling my guitar, but it wouldn't amount to much. Also, I wouldn't get a fair price for it.

We had a hundred-and-twenty bass piano-accordion that we didn't often use. We agreed to sell it for food money, and I was elected salesman. There was a teenage Indian boy who was very interested in the accordion. I took it to him. When I got there he suggested I leave the accordion with him and come back later when his father would be present. Apparently he couldn't do anything during the absence of his old man.

Later, when I got there, I walked right into a family row. The father was giving the son hell for doing things without his knowledge. I was completely ignored while it went on.

'You know I can't stand noisy things!' said the father. 'In fact, I hate musical instruments of any kind. Now here you are, the only son that I have confidence in, actually trying to buy this thing behind my back. What's going to happen to your studies once you get busy keeping the family awake with the noise of this thing?'

Turning to me, he said, 'I'm sorry, friend, but this boy of mine is getting out of hand. He's trying to do things without my consent. And I shall never allow it. This is a respectable family, not a noisy family. Music should be left to snake-charmers. Now, my friend, take your instrument and go. I'm sorry he has wasted your time.' While all this was going on, the boy didn't say a word. He just stood there with his head bowed. I felt sorry for him.

I was struggling to go through the door, bent double under the weight of the accordion, when he called me back.

'Look, my friend,' he said. 'The boy tells me that you people are stranded and need some money. Well, I'm not a bad man at heart. I'll tell you what I can try and do for you. I'll give you five pounds for the instrument to help you out. That's all I can afford. I'm losing because I'm not a music man. I just don't want to see another man suffer.'

So saying, he produced five single notes. He didn't even glance at them. It was as if they were just lying in readiness for this very purpose. Come to think of it, maybe they were. Fearful that he might have a change of heart, I took the money and hurriedly made him out a receipt.

That night my surprise turned to disgust as I stood in the same shop buying food with part of the money he had given me. In a backroom of the shop, I saw the same music-hating old man surrounded by an admiring family of fifteen. He was singing an Indian song in a high-pitched wailing voice to the accompaniment of a wrongly-harnessed accordion.

Ever since that night, I toyed with the idea of meeting that teenage boy in some dark doorway, because something told me that he was in league with his father.

Joe's voice interrupted my dirty intentions. 'Duggie!' he shouted. He was carrying a ten-pound bag of cornmeal and a paperbag full of pork bones. As he unloaded the stuff he said, 'Duggie, we'll never starve again, I found a hole where we can get pork bones bone-cheap.'

'Better tell the boys,' I said, 'in case we need some when you're not around.'

While Brother Joe was explaining the whereabouts of the pork bone hole, I went to the washerwoman for the loan of a pot to cook thick porridge. This kind of porridge not only gives you stamina, it also keeps you fed for quite some time. If my mind wasn't always working overtime, I would have thought of thick porridge, instead of bread, bread. After all, porridge is our staple food. It's cheaper than bread and more filling.

I stirred the porridge, thinking that the Government guards our movements so jealously that I sometimes wonder why we should feel so lost. Christ! I'm glad I'm already mad, otherwise I'd worry about myself. Take these boys, for instance. Not one of them has ever seen the insides of a prison, but just because one rubber stamp is missing from their books, they face a two-year prison sentence at Leeukop where their thighs are going to be used as piss-pots by some long-term convicts.

There was one sure method of getting them to Johannesburg, but it was such a round-about way that it would take a hell of a long time before it could be made to work. The only snag was Zani. If she wasn't so feverish about going home, I could have talked her into remaining with me until a suitable way presented itself. But her itch for home itched worse than the sores on her feet. What made this way unsuitable for Zani was that it was a man's way.

In each large town in South Africa there's an office with a sign board that boasts a picture of a well-built African standing spread-legged and smiling in a miner's uniform. Printed around this impressive picture in bold colourful letters, are the words: 'Native Recruiting Corporation.' The illiterate Africans refer to these offices as the Join because they are the depots where they join, or sign contracts for work in the goldmines in and around Johannesburg. This is one place where they never bother about asking for your pass. Why should they, when you're about to sell yourself for thirty shillings a month? All they do is put a dog label with an engraved number around your neck like they do in the army, then escort you to the mines. After your three-year contract has expired, they escort you back. You're not permitted to wander around.

Now, if I could get Tim and the rest of the boys to agree, I could get them to sign on and then when they get to Johannesburg Station, they could easily give their escorts the slip. Maybe. . . .

'Duggie!'

'Huh?' It was Zani.

'Can't you smell something? The porridge is burning.'

'Sorry, Zani, I was far away.'

'Then come back, man. You're starving us. The boys are impatient, they want to eat and go!'

'Take over, Zani, and leave my share in the pot.'

17

I was happily swinging my artificial leg down the main street of Durban as if there was nothing better in the whole world to have than one leg and two-legged people didn't know what they were missing. It was only when I looked over my shoulder at the taut, naked breasts of those beautiful Zulu maidens who were selling beads to passersby that I swung the leg too fast. The sharp contact of the heel with the cement pavement would send a sharp pain up my thigh and acid words from my lips. I had every reason to be happy, I had at last hit upon a plan of how to get my crowd out of Durban. I stopped at the corner of Field and Smith Streets. This was where the phone-book told me I'd find the social workers' offices.

It didn't take long to tell them the whole story of how we landed in Durban and what had happened ever since. I made a clean breast of everything. After I was through, the nice white lady said, 'Wait a minute, aren't you the boy who lost an artificial leg in Umbilo Park?' I nodded gravely. I didn't want to be reminded of it.

'Sorry,' laughed the social worker as she looked at my gloomy face. 'I can't help laughing whenever I think of that incident.' More seriously she said, 'You do get into strange kind of troubles, don't you?' I swallowed and nodded my head. 'Go to the address where you are staying, I'll see what can be done.' I left, knowing in my heart that something would be done.

The next day the social worker came to the cottage. She told us that she would give us a loan of fifteen pounds and that she'd keep one instrument as security. She assured us that we could take our time in paying the money back. Meantime we needn't worry about the instrument. It would be quite safe.

That night I sighed with relief as the Johannesburg train pulled out of Durban Station. The strains of 'Blues in the Night' from

Tim's trumpet kept mé rooted to the platform until the train was long out of sight.

For me, it was the news van. I wanted to save my ticket money which I was sure I was going to need once I got to Johannesburg. It was Thursday. I had two full days before Sunday. There was nothing for me to do except go back to the cottage.

When I got to the cottage, I found the old washerwoman at home. She was busy cooking on the old stove. I sneaked into the gloomy room, not wishing to meet her. I went straight to my favourite corner and sat down on the floor-boards. I was about to take my artificial leg off and rest my stump, when I heard a soft knock on the door. It was the old lady. Without a word, she bent awkwardly and placed a plateful of thick porridge and meat in front of me.

Straightening up, she said, 'They gone?' I nodded. 'I feel sorry for the girl.' As an afterthought she added, 'And you, too.' She left closing the door softly behind her.

I didn't feel like eating anything. There was nothing that my stomach could take. It was too bloated with defeat. All I wanted was to sit in this gloomy corner and not even think. Tim was right when he said, 'Don't think. Your brains are not to be trusted.'

Everything I touch becomes black sticky liquid, like tar. I had thought the loss of a leg would encourage or somehow force me to lead a serene life. Instead it was the other way around. Pass laws are tough, but pass laws combined with one leg add up to sheer hell.

The bladder in my stomach was still swelling with defeat when Joe came in. He was sweating and out of breath. In his grip was a large suitcase. He dumped it unceremoniously on the floor, and sat heavily next to it. I winced as his buttocks thudded on the floorboards. His fingers started fiddling with his shoe-laces. I got up and opened the window. Brother Joe's feet are noisy enough when reposing in the shoes, but once out of there, they shriek. He kicked them away one after the other. His socks were hopelessly torn. They reminded me of ankleguards, because that was as far as they reached. The ankle. Like soldier's puttees. Between the toes were wet, bluish stains of dirt. Regardless of that, Joe started massaging his toes one by one, as if rubbing the wet stains into the skin.

139

After studying his socks critically, he said, 'You know, Duggie, there are only three things worrying me in this whole world. Socks, underpants and a pass. If I could get those three things, I think I could grow fat. I just wouldn't have a care in the world.'

I sat thinking, 'Joe has very little worries.'

'Mind you, Duggie, it's not the money. I get that now and again just like I got this suitcase.'

Disinterestedly I asked, 'What is it, Joe?'

'It's, it's . . . hell, I don't know,' he said impatiently. 'But everytime I have some money I forget I need these things. They are just not in my mind. I never find myself walking into a shop and telling the shopkeeper to give me a pair of socks and underpants. Just one, Duggie; not many, mind you, just one. Like I do when I go into a shop for cigarettes, or a shebeen for liquor.'

Still without interest, I asked, 'Why, Joe, why can't you go into a shop and buy your own underpants, if they worry you so?'

Musingly he said aloud, 'If someone could snatch my money from me and run into a drapery shop and buy me underpants, maybe that could help.' Still looking at a spot between his toes, he added, 'But I mustn't catch him.'

I spat.

'I just can't understand myself, Duggie.'

'Why?'

Irritably he said, 'You keep on asking why. Isn't that what I want to know? For instance,' he went on, 'when I'm penniless, and my intestines have tied themselves into reef-knots because of hunger, in every shop window I pass, I see all kinds of juicy cold meats and fried fish that have me drooling. But when there's money in my pocket, I don't see these things. They are just not there. You know that upstairs shebeen house in Grey Street before you get to Leopold Street on your right-hand side from the direction of Victoria Street where cane spirits are being sold left and right? At five shillings a quarter?' I shook my head, he was too fast for me.

Ignoring my headshake, he went on, 'There's a drapery shop at the entrance where they sell underclothing dirt cheap. You can get a pair of underpants for as little as two and sixpence. Upstairs is the shebeen. Duggie, you won't believe this, but I never see those underclothes when I go up. I only see them when I come down.

Every time I come downstairs from the shebeen above, I see these underpants. Then I swear on the head of my late mother that the next time I go there, I'll start with the underclothing. But these vacant promises have been going on for six months. Now I've stopped patronising that shebeen because it shows me my true self by dangling what I'm made of right in front of me. No man wants to be shown exactly what he is and that's what that place has done. I can afford a quarter of cane spirits, but I can't afford a pair of underpants. Hell,' he finished off lamely, 'I had to stay away from that place. After all, I've also got a conscience.'

'What's in that suitcase?'

'How the hell should I know? I haven't opened it yet. Had to run like blazes.'

'You don't have to jump down my throat, I was only asking.'

'Sorry, Duggie, for a moment I was feeling bitter with myself. Is the gang gone?'

'Yes, Joe; they pulled out.'

'Good riddance. They were more of a burden to you than a help. Now you and me will be able to think better.'

'There's nothing to think about, Joe, except, maybe, how to get back.'

'Whose plate of food is that, Duggie?'

'Have it, Joe, I just don't feel like anything.'

Joe was wiping the plate with the last bit of porridge, when he screwed up one eye and said, 'It' funny.'

'What's funny?'

'That rickshaw.'

'What rickshaw?'

'The owner of that suitcase.'

'Oh, what about him?'

'He caught me red-handed lifting the suitcase from his cart. I ran like hell down Smith Street with him not far behind, in his hand he had a chumenchu. Why I didn't abandon the suitcase I'll never know, because the damn thing kept on banging on my knee. Anyway, even if there was no suitcase I would never have won the race. Running is the man's daily bread – he earns his living from it.

'But here is the funny part. At the corner of Grey and Smith

Streets I decided to stop trying to outrun a Zulu stallion, and start fighting for my life. I dropped the suitcase and turned. He in turn jumped high up in the air and landed on his haunches reciting the "Thanks of Chaka." They all do that when they are about to put up a good fight.

'Just then, a white policeman came. I was panting heavily.

'"What's going on here?" asks the policeman. The rickshaw dazed me by saying, "It's nothing, baas, was just running." Then he backed away, turned and left me gaping at his muscular bare back. The policeman said, "It didn't seem like nothing to me." Before he could think further, I picked up the suitcase and walked away. This is it. Now can you tell me why the hell the man didn't lay a theft charge on me? After all, it is his suitcase and I did steal the damn thing!'

'I think we better let the suitcase explain,' I said.

'What the hell do you mean let the suitcase explain?' asked Joe densely. 'Suitcases can't talk!'

Calmly I said, 'Open it.'

He did. When he stood back from the open suitcase, he said only one word, and there was disgust in his voice, 'Ganjha!'

Ganjha is the Indian term for the South African drug known as dagga. Marijuana. A few puffs from it could even make your pass book look like a Bible.

'There's your answer.'

'Christ!' said Brother Joe, badly shaken. Beads of perspiration had gathered on his forehead.

'That was a fast-thinking rickshaw, Joe.'

He was staring at the suitcase as if it was full of wriggling snakes.

'Duggie, do you realise that this load is worth five years' hard labour? Plus the four I'm wanted for – hell, my previous convictions plus all this can get me a twenty-year jail term!' The thought made Joe groan. I looked at the stuff and automatically got up to close both the door and window.

'Joe,' I said, 'you see five years' hard labour, I see two hundred and fifty pounds. From where I stand I can tell you that that stuff in that suitcase is first-grade stuff. It will go like butterfly wings in a strong wind.'

'While I go to jail in heavy chains! No, Duggie, take the stuff if you want it, but leave me out of it. Just give me my share after you've got rid of it.'

'O.K., Joe, just do me this one last favour. Take this half-crown and go to the shop at the corner and buy me a small padlock. On your way back, get me a rickshaw.'

'A rickshaw?'

'Yes, Joe, any rickshaw, and I don't want the owner of the case!'

When Joe and the rickshaw came, I loaded the suitcase, and told him to drive me to the hall where our band had enjoyed so many flops. When we got there, I took the suitcase into the hall. I was in luck. The hall was empty.

Behind the stage, leading from one of the dressing-rooms, was a trap door. This door lead into a cellar that was built directly beneath the stage. To see this trap door, you had to take real notice. All I had to do to secure it from intruders was to padlock it. To make double sure, I got Joe to unscrew a red sign from some electrical power house which read: 'Danger. Keep Out.'

Then I started work. I worked until the small hours of the following morning. In spite of my non-stop labour, when morning came, the suitcase was still half full. After counting the small brown paper packets of dagga that I had been folding, I saw that they amounted to four hundred. At a shilling a packet, I had a ready round figure of twenty pounds. That is, if I was not arrested first. Everything seemed like a godsend right up to Hakkeltjie's customers. I knew them all.

Upstairs in the dance hall there were rooms to let at seven and sixpence a week. Now I had a room upstairs with business downstairs. There were many risks, but they were tolerable. Like crossing a street in heavy traffic. When Brother Joe saw my success, he became an active partner. We ordered the drug from as far away as Goleli, the border that divides Swaziland and Natal. We had call-girls who tipped us off whenever foreign seamen wanted the stuff.

The dial of my watch, which was always too slow or too fast, told me it was eight o'clock. Not that I cared, time meant nothing to me. I was just living, and enjoying every minute of it. It was Sunday morning. The dance hall hadn't been swept yet. Evidence of the Zulu choir competition of the night before was strewn all over the dance floor. Cigarette stubs, cold-drink bottles and a womanless stocking, were lying around, the only evidence of a packed gala night.

I was playing 'Danny Boy' strictly by ear on the old battered piano and thinking strictly nothing, when a curious face peeped around the curtain. It must have been peeping for quite some time, because when I looked at it, it smiled mischievously.

I saw the dimples before I saw the smile. When the figure beneath the dimples started toward me, it was as if I was seeing a woman for the first time. Her story was brief and simple. She was a probation nurse from Baragwanath Hospital. She was on her first seaside holiday. Originally, she was from Swaziland, and would I please show her around the town. Hell, three weeks later I found myself before a magistrate monotonously saying, 'I do, I do, I do,' even if it wasn't called for. I was married! Me, Duggie Boetie! What's more, I loved what I married.

With the money I had, we entrained for Johannesburg. After taking her to the hospital where she practised, I went straight to the offices of the British Empire Service League, an organisation that looked after ex-servicemen. Without any difficulty, I was allocated a house at Dube Township under the ex-servicemen's scheme. Then, before returning to Durban to wind up my business, I went to Dube for a last look at my future dwelling. It was really my last look.

Back in Durban, I arrived just in time to hear Brother Joe telling me that the Indian who owned the corner shop wanted two bags urgently. My mind immediately went to furniture money. This being an emergency, me and Joe decided to hire a car for a quick run down to Zululand. We filled a trunk full of the stuff, and packed it in the back seat. Then we filled a sugar bag and loaded it in the boot of the car. It was the first time that we had ever taken the risk of travelling by road. We usually did the runs by train with the help of a fifteen-year-old school girl.

To draw suspicion away from us, we used to dress the girl in school uniform and pack her luggage with the stuff. That way, we were nearly always sure of reaching Durban without any trouble. But this being an emergency, we discarded all formalities. We were zooming past a town called Verulam when the car developed engine trouble. It gave one cough and finally went dead.

That was nothing, no trouble at all, just a bit of engine trouble like any other car. Only this damn car had chosen the queerest of places to conk out.

I don't know who noticed it first: Joe, the Indian driver, or myself. That was not important. The important thing was that directly opposite our car, dutifully flying in the wind, was the Union Jack flag. We were stuck right in front of the Verulam police station.

I don't know who left the car first: Joe, or the Indian driver. But that was not the point. The point was that there they were walking rapidly away. The Indian was trying to catch up on Joe's rapid strides, but Joe wouldn't let him. Soon they broke into a run. Again I was left holding the baby.

Slowly I got out of the car. To my relief the pavement was empty. There wasn't a soul that mattered. Except for an Indian woman carrying the broadest basket I had ever seen on the crook of her arm. The street was as deserted as the broad step that led up to the police station.

I was about to follow the two cowards, when the corner of my eye caught sight of the trunk in the back seat. Greed took over. I stood rooted to the spot. This is how Jeegar must have felt when he tried to drive that Chinese car away to safety against terrible odds. Then two of my life-long corns appeared at the top of the stone steps in the form of uniformed police.

I left the car door wide open on purpose hoping that the air would clear the dagga smell inside. Then I crippled boldly up the stairs towards my legal guardians. When I was three steps away from them, I looked up and said in faultless Afrikaans, 'Baas, my car doesn't want to start.' One of them looked up at the other and grinned. He took a match box out of his trouser pocket and made as if to give it to me. The one said, 'What's wrong my boy?'

I shrugged my shoulders, still in Afrikaans I said, 'I don't know, baas.'

'Come,' he said to his friend, 'let's see if we can't help this boy.' His friend looked at the palms of his spotless pink hands, and shook his head.

The policeman didn't bother to close the car door as he tried the starter of the car. It whined like a hoarse child, but wouldn't catch. He tried it again with the same results. In the meantime, the dagga in the car was smelling like a witch doctor's burning headgear, or so it seemed to me. I stopped inhaling in case I panicked and gave the game away. The blocked air in my lungs nearly caused me to black out.

Hurriedly, I took a cigarette out of my pocket and started puffing furiously on it, hoping to kill the dagga smell with smoke from my cigarette. Maybe his nostrils were blocked like most of the white race. I didn't know, but I hoped so. He got out of the car, and opened the bonnet. Then I really started pulling on the cigarette. After bending for a few minutes over the gaping bonnet, he straightened up and whistled amazed. 'Kosie,' he called. 'Come here and take a look.' I got out of the smoke filled car and had a look with Kosie. The constable pointed at the carburettor. It was chockful of sand.

'No wonder your car wouldn't move. Take that out and clean it. I'm not going to dirty my hands. Then pump some petrol into it and we'll see if she won't start. When you're finished, call me.'

When I was through, I signalled to him again. He got into the car. This time he closed the door. While I started saying my prayers the car started with a roar. He released the clutch and it shot forward at a reckless speed. He let her go for five hundred yards, then he stepped on the brakes hard. After that he reversed with the same speed. Getting out of the car he said, 'Careful next time.'

'Dankie, baas,' I stammered. I still couldn't believe that the man didn't smell anything.

I got into the car and used my left hand to place my artificial leg on the clutch. I pushed the artificial knee down with the palm of my hand until the clutch was flat against the floor boards, then I pulled the gear out of neutral and into first. After that I eased the pressure from the palm of my left hand slowly. I felt the clutch lift and I lowered the gas pedal slowly with my right foot. The car moved.

While all this was going on, the policeman up the stairs was wondering why was I taking so long to get going. He was just about to come down the stairs when the car moved.

Once the car was on the go, I was all right because I didn't need the services of my left leg. My right leg did all the necess-

146

ary press work. I reached Durban without mishap.

I've never seen two men so surprised as Joe and the Indian when they saw me the following morning. I told them that the police had taken the drugs for themselves and had allowed me to go. The hell with it, didn't they run out on me? The Indian was too relieved at getting his car back to bother about the charges. As for Brother Joe, he resigned on the spot. Next I heard from him, he was selling corn beer at the Victoria Street beer hall. A much safer business, as he put it. All he did was buy a pound's worth of corn beer and sit around in the beer hall till the beer tanks closed. Then the latecomers bought it from him at twice the price.

I was in my room, sitting spread-legged on the floor. In front of me was an old newspaper. It was strewn with dagga. My last bag. After this, I intended washing my hands of the business. At my elbow, within easy reach, was a bottle of brandy. It was three-quarters full. This brandy was not for drinking purposes. It was there to make third-grade dagga into first-grade. You spread the dagga out before you like it was now, then you sprinkled a little brandy on it. The spirits shrunk the stuff. When it was dry, there'd be hard little knots. At the same time, the colour changed from green to a reddish-green. In other words, from third-grade to first-grade.

I wasn't around. Only my nimble fingers were. They were fast rolling the stuff into little parcels while my mind was at Baragwanath Hospital. First time I ever believed in witchcraft. That nurse had me. I was like somebody possessed. To me she was my mother, my father, my only friend, all wrapped in one.

That was why when someone tapped me on the shoulder, I payed him no mind. Not until an authoritative voice nearly broke my eardrums by barking, 'Get up!' I looked over my shoulder, and my breath became hot. My stomach muscles contracted and my mouth behaved like a fish that had just been landed.

When things like these start happening, confusion sets in fast. Otherwise there would be a lot more dead policemen in the world. You become too bewildered to think straight. It was one of those times when you fight till your arms fall off, or you become a complete idiot. I became the latter.

I was so engrossed with thoughts of my wife, that one of the most important things escaped my mind. Namely, to bolt the door from the inside, and have a lock hanging from the outside. 'Mister! This is a police raid!'

I was hauled to prison, where I was kept three months awaiting trial while they checked my previous convictions.

This all goes to show the part the police play in my life. It has been going on ever since I was born, and it will go on till I die. They are out to ruin me, always have. This time they succeeded.

Like all the magistrates that I have come across, he found me guilty. After preaching me a sermon about the behaviour of cripples, he sentenced me to three years and three months. Three years for dagga, and three months for the brandy. When I asked him to waive the three months, he pointed at my pile of records and told me that was the reason why I awaited trial so long.

18

What was three and a quarter years even in a place like Intaba Zo Sizi (Mountain of Sorrow), my new jail, when my mind was forever on the woman I loved.

I was in group A, with the staff job at reception. I was not going to start any trouble, because I was no longer irresponsible. I had a wife to think of.

The prison was divided into three sections. A, B and D. They start you off in A section. B stands for bad, from there it's D prison for you. D means dangerous, or 'Hyenas' Cage'. The inmates of D section are real inmates. They were never allowed out. As a result, any kind of smuggling was out of the question. Their favourite pastime was to kill one another off. Me, I was going to do my utmost not to grace that section with my presence.

It was the longest prison term I ever pulled in my life. My five years at the Fort was nothing compared to Intaba Zo Sizi. Here, minutes were like hours, hours like days. I suppose the tortoise pace was caused by my being in love.

Maybe I should have written to her, I don't know. But I didn't want her to know that she was married to a reformed criminal.

Since meeting her, I knew deep down that I had reformed. These thoughts sped through my mind as I stood, a free man, outside the big prison gates waiting for the prison truck to haul me to Durban Station.

My three years were served to the full; I didn't do the three months, thanks to remission and good behaviour. I took a last look at the formidable iron doors and unconsciously read the three chalk words that were written boldly on them: 'Kilroy was Here'. Kill-joy would have been more appropriate, I thought, as I spat and walked away without waiting for the prison truck.

As the train carrying me back to Johannesburg and home rumbled through the Italian prisoner of war tunnels near Pietermaritzburg, I couldn't resist looking at my reflection in the compartment mirror. The hair on my head was scraped clean by the convict barber, giving me the look of a hairless pink monkey.

At Johannesburg Station I got off the train and made my way to the station's butcher just in case there was no food at home. After all, nobody was expecting me. There was a lot of confusion on the platform. People were running up and down, especially old ladies with washing bundles and babies tied on their backs. They were jumping into the wrong trains then jumping out of them again, only to find they had jumped from the right train. They kept asking people who didn't know either but were too proud to admit the fact. A mess of human frustration, pushing, pulling, and tramping on one another as they fought to get into the narrow single doors. The loudspeaker that was announcing the destination of the train succeeded only in giving a fair imitation of a horse being slaughtered. A hell of a bedlam.

As a train was being mobbed, I asked a struggler where it was going to. He said Nancefield. A girl's voice behind me said, 'You're mad; this is a Dube train.' The man shrugged his shoulders and pushed. A woman next to him screamed, at the same time the guard's warning whistle shrilled. The train started to move while people were still dangling outside. A teenager who was trying to get in through the window had succeeded only with the top half of his body. Inside, the train was so crowded that it was as if someone had added more sardines to an already packed tin, and was trying to reclose the tin. I pushed through. The

149

vacant seat I found was worth the two missing buttons on my jacket.

On nearing Braamfontein Station, a surprising thing happened. Occupants of seats started getting up. I thought they had reached their destination. Instead, they climbed on to their seats and stood on them. To me this was unusual. I always thought it was better to sit than to stand. I was not going to follow any mob psychology. The result was near disaster. At Braamfontein Station, the train was again mobbed. This time, in real earnest. Maybe it was because Braamfontein is an industrial area.

Funny, when you're in distress, your mind wanders over irrelevant things. There I was thinking of industrial areas when I was slowly suffocating to death.

Suddenly there was an eclipse. I looked up, then blinked. My head was under a woman's skirt. I saw big buttocks covered by white bloomers. Hastily I looked down, not wanting to smell anything in case there was something to smell. This nightmare journey took three quarters of an hour. When at last we reached Dube Station, I staggered, minus my walking-stick, dazedly out of the train, vowing never to board a train again, even if it was going to fairyland.

I looked at my watch with distrust, and saw that it was five-thirty. I shrugged my shoulders and started to walk home. I transferred the flat parcel of meat from my right hand to my left to sort of balance the weight, since my walking-stick was gone. My progress was painfully slow, but I couldn't have cared less, since I'd soon be resting.

A big lock on my gate kept me from entering the yard. I hadn't bargained for this. It was all adding confusion to an already confused mind. I looked around, then decided to enquire at the next house. I was just about to walk away, when I saw someone familiar walking toward me. I waited, at the same time wondering where had I seen him before. I was leaning against the gate. It was a good thing I did, otherwise I would have fallen. Because I had never laid eyes on the man before: what was familiar was the suit he had on. It was mine. My wedding suit! It was cut by a West Street tailor just before my marriage. My best and only suit. The last time I had seen it, it was neatly folded and resting at the bottom of my wife's trunk.

Now here was someone dressed to kill in it. I wasn't mad, or even angry, or any of those things. Just a little foolish. As usual, when I was being deeply hurt, my bowels wanted to work. The slight headache that I had had since getting off the train, suddenly became a splitting headache.

'Hello!' he said.

'Hello!' I said, conscious of a slight tremor in my voice. He whipped out a key ring from the side pocket of his (my) jacket, and started unlocking the lock.

'Can I help you?'

'No. Yes. Where can I get a drink?' That was all I could think of saying.

He laughed, 'Not here!'

The gate opened. I limped aside.

'You look tired,' he said.

I nodded, paralysed.

He looked closely at me. 'Come in, have a rest. We don't sell drink, but I can get it for you.' He had a nice pleasant face with strong white teeth – no prison teeth like mine. He helped me inside. I just stood. My lips couldn't speak. 'Sit down,' he said. 'I won't be a minute.'

From where I sat, I could see into the bedroom. He took off my jacket, I mean ours, then he hung it in a wardrobe. He stopped at the door and looked closely at me again. I was scared he might have seen a photograph. But I was very thin now, and without my hair.

'Can I give you some water?' he asked. I shook my shiny head. 'Well, what can I do for you then?'

It was a trembling hand that passed over the money to him.

'A nip of brandy, please.'

'I won't be long. I have to get my children from the woman who looks after them during the day. My wife is a staff-nurse. She should be here any minute. But don't worry, just make yourself at home. I'll be back before her.' With that, he was gone.

Make yourself at home, the man had said. But this was my home. I got up to go and have another look at the number. Maybe it was the wrong number. Sure enough, it was my number. Thirteen-o-two. As I reoccupied my seat, all kinds of thoughts sped through my mind. I thought maybe this was my wife's cousin, or maybe it was her brother, or . . . oh, hell.

I looked around more carefully. A wedding photograph. My wife. My suit. There the relationship ended. Stuck in at the base of the wedding picture was a picture of two kids. One about eighteen months old, the other about six months. The older one looked like a boy. The exact replica of my wife. My bowels wanted to work. This time it was even worse. I started to cry. And that doesn't come easily to me. I thought I heard someone coming and rubbed at my face, but it was just a woman passing. I got to the door and climbed out cautiously. No him, no kids, no staff-nurse. I just walked and walked not caring the hell where I was going, cursing myself, cursing him, cursing her, cursing the whole damn world. Despite myself I couldn't help seeing it her way. She marries a man. He's an angel for three weeks. He goes back to Durban to wind up some business and then he doesn't show up again. So she waits and she hunts and she waits. Still no husband. So she meets up with this smiling saint and it's sweet dreams, Duggie. Most probably adverts in the *Bantu Earth* and *Natal Moon*, which is the beginning of divorce proceedings. And while I'm still cuddling my scruples in jail my suit gets married again.

The sharp hoot of a car jerked me from my misery, and with a jeering finger showed me my surrounding hell. I found myself at the bottom step of the bridge that led to Dube Station's platform. Sighing with self-pity, I started mounting them painfully, without my walking-stick. My entire body was screaming for a rest and the Dube beer hall would do me good.

I roamed around the beer hall in the hope of seeing someone I knew. But luck was against me. I bought myself a shilling's worth of beer and perched myself on a bench. Now there was my rotten pass book to worry about. Nothing short of a lighted match could fix it.

I sat on the corner bench slowly sipping my drink, when I heard the drummer. He was standing directly in front of me, as dirty and nauseating as ever. More and more bad luck. It was the mad teacher. There was pus as thick as condensed milk at both corners of his eyes. I avoided the face and looked away. Maybe in six months time I'd be just like him. If only he'd go away.

Abruptly the drum stopped beating and I heard him say, 'I crave for your wisdom and hate your scorn . . . I pray for guidance with hope forlorn . . .'

He started beating on his drum holding it close to his ear and whispering and blowing on it. Not one of the drinkers were taking notice of his ravings. For that matter, I don't think he did either.

I was about to take my mug of beer and move away when someone near me shouted, 'Hey, you! *Futsek* away from here, we want to drink.' He walked away singing 'Nkosi Sikelele e Africa'.

I was about to put the mug down between my legs after having taken a deep drink, when I saw Zala, a string bass player. We had once shared the back of a police van together after being arrested for being without night specials.

I went over to him and glanced at the newspaper over his shoulder. There was a state of emergency declared in South Africa. My eyes travelled away from there to the crime column. I noticed Zala's eyes were also there.

'Zala,' I said.

He spun round, 'Christ! Duggie, where the hell've you been? The last I heard of you was when you and Tim toured Durban! How did it go? Tell me, man, how did it go?'

'First tell me whether you can put me up for the night.'

'Sure, Duggie, but I'm not at Orlando anymore. I'm now at a place called Naledi.'

'Where the hell is that?'

'About an hour's ride from town and twenty minutes from here.'

As we got off the train at Naledi, Zala became unusually quiet.

'What's eating you, boy?'

'Huh?'

'Why so quiet—'

'I'm thinking, Duggie, thinking of that stone.'

'What stone?'

'It's getting on my nerves.'

'What are you talking about?'

'Never mind, you'll see.'

It was late when we got to Zala's house. His young wife met us at a fenceless gate. I noticed the area was newly built. The whole place, as far as you can see, was rocky. Inside, there were four doorless unplastered rooms. As usual, the lavatory was built a distance from the house. There was no bathroom.

When I entered the fourth room, I stopped and gaped. In the middle of the room was a huge boulder. A channel was built around it. Next to the boulder stood a fire-galley. It made the tiny room unbearably hot. On the fire-galley, about to boil, was a four-gallon tin of water.

Zala said, 'This is the rock that gives me sleepless nights. The rock of Gibraltar. Duggie, I sweat morning and night trying to get rid of it. You see that channel I built around it? Someone advised me to continually throw boiling water around it to get it to crack.'

'But how did it get here?' I asked, amazed.

'It didn't get here, it was here. The house got here. I mean, they built the house around it.'

'Why don't you report this matter to the superintendent?' I asked.

'I did. The bastard told me to carve a table out of it.'

I wanted to laugh, but it wasn't funny.

'They build these houses so fast, you'd think they use a magic wand. You leave a vacant plot to go to work, when you come back, you find a house.' There was disgust in Zala's voice.

'I've been fighting this boulder for a week with a sure feeling that I'm losing. All the wood and coal I'm buying and carrying is making me physically weak and financially broke.'

'What made you leave Orlando Township?'

'I didn't leave, I was elbowed out. I lived in Orlando Township all my life. That house was what you call an inheritance; I took it over when my parents died. It had a bathroom, with hot and cold water, and a kitchen sink and house gutters and cement right round the yard. Then one morning I was summoned to the superintendent's office. He told me I must make way for people who get less wages and go to a new township – Moroka – where the rent was higher. When I pointed out the money I had spent to make the place look decent, he told me that the house didn't belong to me, that it was Government property. And as for the improvements on the house, they were done at my own risk.

'Hell, Duggie, we were hardly three months at Moroka Township when I was kicked out of my job. A good job. I was locked up twice at Kliptown police station for being hopelessly behind with my rent. I was transferred to Jabavu. There the houses are worse, Duggie. They are built Siamese-fashion. If your bed-springs squeak, the family next door hears. If you quarrel with your wife, you have to quarrel in whispers. What nearly drove my wife mad was the wood and coal smoke from the next house.

'You see, the walls that divide the two families don't go right up to the ceiling. They go half-way. So when the family in the next house makes a fire, we get at least half their smoke. Hell, Duggie, maybe we are not civilised yet, but we are more civilised than these houses!

'Then my luck changed. I got a better paying job. The first thing I wanted to do was to go to the superintendent's office and ask him for permission to extend those walls up to the ceiling to keep the smoke out. But my wife said nix. No more money was going to be spent on a house that didn't belong to us. Not when we might be told to get out any time. She was right. When the superintendent found out that I was earning four pounds a week, he transferred me to where I am now. If I lose this job . . .' his voice trailed off. 'I tell you, Duggie, what a black man needs is a caravan. If the man says go, you go, man. But I'm boring you with my house difficulties. Tell me about Durban. What happened there?'

'Tomorrow,' I sighed, 'or the next day. For now, just show me a little piece of floor.'

'Seriously, what are you going to do now, Duggie?'

'Try and get this hopeless pass fixed, I think.'

'Let me see.' I gave it to him. He thumbed through it, then gave it back to me.

'What do you think of it?'

'Nothing.'

'What do you mean, nothing?'

'I mean it stinks.'

'O.K. Now, where's that piece of floor?'

19

Next morning I was at Influx. I was careful not to show the police guards at the gate my pass. Upstairs at the social workers' offices I was told that things were different now. They told me to try and get a doctor's certificate. But I wasn't sick, I told them, I was in prison, and there were my prison discharge papers. 'Yes, we see them,' said the man, 'but where were you before you went to prison?' I'd often heard about questions that can't be answered. This was one of them.

I took my battered pass and prison papers and went downstairs. There I took a chance and went directly to the work-seeking permit officer, thinking that he might take pity on my being legless. He took one look at my pass and personally shouted 'Escort!' before I could even blubber. The beginning of the end, I thought.

While he was holding on to my pass, I reversed, meaning to lose myself in the black throngs of misery. I would have succeeded if I hadn't tramped on somebody's corn while reversing. He took it upon himself to push me forward into the hands of the escort. It was hopeless to try and run. Hell, what am I talking about? Running had been long out of the question for me.

'I wonder what caused him to do it? I saw him only a few minutes before he did it, and he seemed happy and cheerful.' What they don't know is that the reason why you've been so happy the last few minutes is because you have at last pounced on the only way out. You wonder why you didn't think of it before. You are going to smite your miserable life to death, and enjoy every minute of it. It's your secret and yours alone. You giggle when you think of it. You're as smug as a hanged man at the end of a rope. People believe that there's a mysterious happiness in the last hours of a dead man's life. But it's not for them to know, because the secret belongs to the dead. They regard death as an unfair evil. What they don't seem to understand is that only death can play a noble part when endurance is exhausted.

All this was passing through my mind as I was escorted upstairs to the prosecutor's interrogating room. The policeman knocked and opened the door. He clicked his heels smartly and motioned me to enter. He gave my pass to a tall white man, then came and stood next to me.

'Now, what's this?' he began, as he scrutinised my pass. He looked up at me and said to the policeman, 'Why bring him here, why not lock him up? This book is hopeless, man.'

The policeman said, 'Is cripple, sir.'

Irritably he said, 'That doesn't mean anything.'

Turning to me he said, 'Where are you cripple?'

'One leg, sir.'

He stood up to have a better look.

Then, 'I see two.'

'Artificial, sir,' I said, knocking on the leg.

'What happened?'

'War!'

He coughed and directed his attention back to my pass. Musingly he said, 'I see here you've only worked once – why?'

'It's difficult for a man like me to find a job.'

'Why?'

' 'Cause I got no leg.'

'Nonsense, you're just lazy, that's all.'

'Not lazy. It's painful and discouraging to walk every day to the pass office only to be told there's no work.'

'Don't talk nonsense; I say you're lazy.' Banging his fist on the desk, he said angrily, 'I don't accept that excuse! I happen to know men in worse positions than you are, going through life without a complaint!'

Good for them, I thought.

'Have you ever heard of Lieutenant Bader?' I nodded. We used to hear in camp about the legless British ace's exploits. How he was a prisoner of war and how they flew his two artificial legs to him from England and dropped them by parachute over the German prison camp.

'Well,' said the prosecutor, whom I was slowly beginning to dislike, 'I was in the Air Force myself, and I happened to know Bader personally. Legless as the lieutenant is, he never made capital of his disability. The man used to walk around and dance

157

with his artificial legs. Yet you with the advantage of one, have the nerve to tell me that you find walking with an artificial leg difficult!'

I heard myself reply, 'Sir, in the first place, Lieutenant Bader has expensive legs. Not legs that weigh fifteen to twenty pounds and produce blisters every second week. Secondly, he is well-off, and last of all, he doesn't have to walk up and down the streets trying to fix a pass. I'll change places with him any time!'

'Have you ever been to prison?'

'Huh?'

'Have you ever been to prison?'

'What's that got to do with this?'

'Look, I'm asking the questions. Have you ever been to prison?' I looked down and nodded. When I looked up, he was grinning.

'Look,' he said, wiping the grin off his face, 'I'm going to deal with the man in you, not with your crippleness. That has nothing to do with me. My business is you! If you can prove to my satisfaction where you've been since leaving your last place of employment, I'll see what I can do for you, and not before.'

'But that was years ago.'

'I don't care whether it was one week ago. I'll give a two-week special, and if you are ever brought before me again, without documents, *ek sal jou gal werk!* Now get out of here!'

Slowly I made my way to the station to catch the Dube train. I was going to the beer hall to think, and there was no suicide in my thoughts. I'd been in tighter spots than this. As I climbed the steps that led from the station's platform to the bridge and the beer hall, I saw them. Pass raiders. The fresh two-week stamp special in my pass book allowed me to ignore them.

Two hours later, I was still wondering whether this was really the kind of life I was cut out for. Homeless, passless, and legless. And suddenly I knew what I was going to do. I stood up sweating, my beer half-finished.

I took a train to Pretoria, capital of the Transvaal. There, I was directed to the bus rank. I boarded one to the Union Buildings. I walked up three flights of stairs. When I came to the third floor, an arrow sign drawn on a board directed me to the Coloured Identification Department. Win, lose, there was no draw possible. I was taking the bull by the horns. This time there was no going back, for man or mouse.

At the office entrance, there was a long bench. It was empty. Worriedly I perched on it. From inside the office came hilarious laughter. That made me a little nervous. My courage threatened to desert me. I gripped the bench tightly so as not to bolt and run. The laughter inside continued uproariously. At least they are happy, I thought, that's something.

I wasn't there long before a burly white man came out of the happy office and stood at the door. He was red in the face from laughter, and wiping his eyes with a khaki handkerchief. He looked up and down the long corridor. Then he saw me. Controlling himself with difficulty, he said in Afrikaans, 'You – come here.' I followed him meekly into his office.

He pointed to a figure that sat squirming in a chair. Before he could say anything, he burst into laughter. He was joined by two others. I looked at the figure on the chair, and saw a pitch-black man. His shoes were worn out. After controlling himself, the white man said, 'Boy –' it sounded like 'Booy'. 'Now you tell me, boy, does this man look like a Coloured to you?' Again there was laughter. I looked at the poor man and felt sorry for him.

'Come on,' urged the Afrikaner. 'Does he now, does he?'

I was about to say, 'I don't know, baas.' Then I remembered my own position, and through my mind flashed the story of the monkey. I looked at the man and I grinned. My grin was not beautiful. It must have been ugly, because it brought forth more laughter.

A pet monkey once followed the aroma of frying peanuts into its master's kitchen. There, strewn on the hot stove, were the frying nuts. He looked around, to make sure that there was no one around. Then he reached out with his paw. As the tips of his fingers made contact with the hot plate, he screamed, somersaulted and sucked his scorched fingers. He tried again, with the same results. He was still sucking his poor fingers and trying to scratch out an idea from the crown of his head with the fingernails of his left hand, when the cat came in. At the sight of the cat, the monkey grinned. In one swift move he snatched the cat up, and with it swiped the strewn nuts from the hot stove. The cat screamed and bolted through the door. Grinning, the monkey started picking up the nuts leisurely from the floor. I was sorry, but I was going to do to this man what the monkey did to the cat.

Spacing each word, and in faultless Afrikaans, I said, 'If you, my friend, as black as you are, claim to be a Coloured, then what the hell should I claim to be?' From the top pocket of my jacket I pulled out a pencil.

'Here, take this pencil, and push it through your hair. If the pencil goes through without a hitch, then the baas will issue you with Coloured clearance papers, but if the pencil sticks in your hair, then you're nothing but a kaffir.'

The office vibrated with laughter.

'Yeh, yeh!' they screamed. 'Go on, take the pencil. Yes, yes,' continued the voices.

The poor man made no move. That uncombed bush of crinkly hair could have gripped a broom stick. As for a pencil, it could have lived there for years.

'Yes, yes, stick the pencil through your hair. If it falls off, we'll issue you with a Coloured pass.' If eyes could kill, I would have died where I stood. Still laughing, the baas said, 'Here is a man who could claim to be Coloured. Just look at his complexion, I'm sure if there was a hair on his head, the hair would have been straight.'

My smooth-shaven head was once more coming to my rescue. In Cape Town, I wanted to have my drinks in a pub that catered for Coloureds only. Africans were prohibited from drinking in pubs. I knew that if I tried entering one, I'd only be thrown out because of my crinkly hair.

For a solution I went to a barber and told him to remove my hair. 'All?' he asked surprised.

'All,' I assured him. After the hair-cut I went to the pub. I pushed open one bat-wing door and held it until I was sure that the bartender's eyes were centred on me. Instead of going in, I turned my head towards the street and swore volubly at an imaginary molester using juicy rude words like a real Cape Malay. Then I pushed both doors open and danced a jig towards the counter. 'A glass of sherry.' I ordered. And was served. From then on, I was a regular customer. But from the way the barman eyed me every time I entered the pub, I knew that he was waiting for my hair to grow, so as to see whether it was crinkly or straight. He was going to wait a long time, because I was equally anxious to see that it didn't grow.

The baas behind me said, 'Now stop wasting our time and get out of here before we have you locked up.' Shakily the man got off the chair and walked toward the door. I didn't meet his eyes, I knew how Judas felt.

'You!' The voice was directed at me. I braced myself. 'I suppose you also want a Coloured identification card?'

'Yes, baas.'

'Where were you all the time, that you want one now? Why didn't you come before?'

'Before, baas, it wasn't so important, but now it is very important that I should have some kind of paper to say who I am.'

'So you want to know who you are?'

'Yes, baas.'

He grinned. 'Who the hell are you anyway?'

'Duggie Boetie, baas.'

'Why is it so important now, when you've been going without it all your life?'

'It's because I want to marry, baas,' I stammered and looked down.

'Marry!' he exclaimed. 'Who wants to marry a cripple?'

'I think it's because she's twenty years older than me, baas,' I said shamelessly.

The office exploded with laughter. 'So that's the case, heh?' he said, wiping his eyes. When the din had subsided, he turned to the young one and said, 'Take down his particulars and give him a temporary form to go with until we can issue him with a real identification card.'

Turning to me he said, 'Next time you come here, bring two passport photos with you . . .'

Two passport photos. And I was a Coloured. Just like that. I limped out in a daze. My head was spinning, my heart was double-timing and my ears were going ping. I wanted to sing or dance or something. I wanted to fly. I needed my guitar. No more pass! No more pass! No more Influx Control! No more sit here, not there, no more shut up, take your hands out of your pockets, no more where the hell do you think you're going, no more you are a liar, do you know who you're talking to, no more move,

161

wait, line up, fall in, no more can't you see I'm busy – No more! No more! It was now somebody else's shit – everybody else's – not mine! I wanted to start shaking hands, banging everybody on the back, buying booze for the whole of bloody Joburg! I looked around wildly.

Standing forlornly at the building's entrance was the unfortunate black man.

My hand fished into my pocket and came out with a shilling. I went to him and placed the shilling in his hand, then quickly walked away. I was a few hundred yards from him, when something flew with terrific force past my head. It went *zinnnnng*, narrowly missing the tip of my ear. It clinked once and fell into the gutter. It was the shilling piece. I bent down, picked it up and walked on without looking back.

Epilogue

This book was meant to be the first volume of the autobiography of Dugmore Boetie. Now I don't know what it is. A book, certainly. A book covering years (early 'thirties to early 'fifties) that he knew, and set mostly in places that he knew.

Duggie was, by his own definition, a con man; so that attempts I have made to establish the facts of his life have led only to chaos and contradiction. Just yesterday I spoke to somebody who claims to have been a student of a sort of Duggie Boetie school for junior thieves. Then, in contrast, there was the lovely young African nurse in Zululand, where I took Duggie to die, who gasped and wept when she saw him: 'I know this man – from Johannesburg! I grew up under him! He used to play the guitar for us when we were children – he used to tell us stories!'

I met Duggie roughly two years before he died. Which is about how long it took for the first draft of this book to be written. It was some time in 1964. I was running an improvisation group of African and white actors and writers. We attempted to investigate, through improvisations and monologues, the everyday encounters between us. Not the dramatic ones; the seemingly simple ones, where the convolutions were as complex, the poisons as insidious.

'The Last Leg,' an edited version of what is now Chapter 14, had appeared as a short story in *The Classic*, a largely black literary magazine. It excited many people. The then editor of *The Classic*, the late Nat Nakasa, was a very lively member of our improvisation group, and I asked him to bring Duggie along. He did.

Duggie was small, dapper, vivacious, sharp. He carried a walking stick which helped compensate for an artificial leg. At improvisation, he was inventive, unobvious, bold. He filled the place with his presence, his anecdotes. Nat, sophisticated, urbane, was irritated by him; the rest of us were fascinated, relishing all the rogue that showed. He claimed seventeen criminal convictions in his time and to have lost his leg in the Sahara, serving against Rommel.

Ruth First, the political activist and author, was newly released from 117 days of solitary confinement. I showed her "The Last Leg" and, deeply moved, she asked to meet Duggie. When we both reiterated our admiration for his story, he put forward a proposition. If we *really* admired his work, he had to ask, what were we going to do about it? Working at a radio factory, travelling to and from Germiston every day with an artificial leg exhausted him, made writing virtually out of the question. If we could provide him 'just with a roof over his head, food and paper for three months', he would write the 'true, hot book' that was 'bursting to come out'.

When I took reasonably to his request, he adjusted it swiftly. A roof, food, paper and, say, £15 a month. Finally I committed myself to matching his present wage, £30 a month, for three months by collecting from friends as well as myself. He was to write what he liked.

After about six weeks, he came to see me with some pages of manuscript, about an African gang of criminals which had somehow ended up in the army. After the war, each returned to South Africa with a single purpose – to beat the others to hidden loot. In trying to reach it, they all get killed, one by one, through the most extraordinary fates. One died by shark, another by his mother . . . Beside the humour, irony and originality of 'The Last Leg,' this was thin. The influences were obvious: comics, movies, Agatha Christie, Peter Cheyney. What was marvellously, uniquely Duggie hadn't even been touched on. We discussed it extensively, passionately. I explained that this kind of writing was valid in itself, and that if it was what he wanted to do he might quite easily get good support. But that it was not writing that interested me, that I truthfully did not know enough about it to help in any way.

I quoted Dickens – *David Copperfield*. Begin with 'I was born,' I said.

'Do you want it *all*?' Duggie asked. 'As it was? All the shit?' I assured him that I did. 'We'll get into trouble,' he said. I asked him to tell what he knew, what mattered to him, as best, as simply, as truthfully as he could. Then we'd worry about trouble. So he began again. Not with 'I was born . . .' but a kind of equivalent.

At about this time, Nat Nakasa was given a Nieman Scholarship for a year's study at Harvard University. He was not permitted a passport, so he left on an exit permit. This meant that he could never return to South Africa under the present regime. At his request, I took over the editorship of *The Classic*. Some months later, Nat committed suicide in New York.

Soon after the Rivonia trials, it was politically a difficult time. I earned my living as an advertising copy-writer. Very few people in the agency knew about my theatrical or literary activities. Duggie used to come to the office. Not *into* the office, but to the downstairs foyer of the building. The watchman used to come up and call me. I used to go down, receive the new manuscript and give back the old one. With questions. Opening questions, I hope; I tried not to intrude, only to provoke.

We had many meetings in that pale, marble-faced foyer or, when it was cold, out in the winter sun on the pavement. The three months extended themselves and the book was barely begun. I got more money. After five months, the book was just halfway there and I was supporting him on my own. When the money came regularly, Duggie didn't write regularly. I knew that in many ways I was just another con to him. This was fine, as long as a book was happening. He sometimes stayed away for a whole month. I kept him going, which meant that the visits and the writing became more regular. God knows what Dugmore's life was; I only know what he told me. There was a woman he lived with who he said was mad and beat him. There was the difficulty of having a place to write in peace. He had no family, just a dead sister's children who were being looked after by an old woman he had to give money to. Often he smelt of brandy. Once a job interview was arranged for him and he arrived drunk. And there was that leg, that I watched from afar sometimes, heavy, stiff and cruel, that seemed to propel the rest of him like a punting pole.

I decided to get him to complete the book, imperfectly, and then work back. With a sense of pattern, of a whole, it might be easier to sustain his interest. It wasn't the end of what he wanted to say, but it could be the first volume. He completed it, ending off with: OK BARNEY – HERES MY WRATH! We had been working so close to things that I had lost perspective. Seeing the book as a whole was a revelation. It was magnificently vital, funny, strong and ironic at its best. Hopelessly sentimental and inaccurate when he attempted to care. There was a lot to question, a lot of work to do.

And then suddenly Duggie, without money, disappeared. I waited for about three weeks and then began to search for him. After a month, he phoned me. He had been sick. His right arm, the one above his stump, was going into violent spasms. He was coughing badly. He thought that he had pneumonia and was going to hospital. Duggie had two passes: one issued to Africans; the other a 'Coloured' identity card. The first because he preferred to live among Africans, the second to get the privileges that came with it. He chose the superior attention of the Coronationville Hospital.

Then began a new ritual; visiting Duggie in hospital. He had no family. His friends seemed to have forgotten him. I went twice a week after work. His arm, except for occasional spasms, was now virtually immobile. He lay and dreamt about sour milk and pigs' knuckles, and so I brought them to him. At first he was relatively cheerful. We discussed things. Shoes. He was going to get a £20 pair of American Freeman shoes when he left the hospital. Food. I remember once listening to him boast about how splendid a cook he was. He could cook a seven-course dinner. 'A seven-course dinner?' I asked. Duggie and crêpe suzettes. I leaned back indulgently while he listed the seven. 'Meat. Potatoes. Beans. Pumpkin. Rice. Carrots. Cabbage. Even more.'

As soon as he was better he would finish off the book. It needed some juggling, some rewriting, a fortnight or so's work. I brought him books, but he never read; paper, but he never wrote. It was summer. The ward was hot. Radios were loud. Pop music. Commercials. Two beds away from him was a tiny, toothless, legless old man making rugs. He had a thin, piercing voice, a wild cackle, and yelled at people far across the ward. Duggie hated him, said that he was cruel, that he mocked and frightened the very sick.

Duggie's condition seemed to worsen. I went to speak to the doctor in charge of his ward. Duggie had cancer of the lung; it had spread, affecting his arm. He wasn't sure how long Duggie would live. Perhaps months. A year. They took him once a week to the General Hospital for radium treatment. The doctor advised against telling Duggie. One can never predict exactly how a patient might react. His condition, however, would reach a kind of plateau of comfort when he would quite likely be able to work again.

So my ritual became more significant. Sometimes Nadine Gordimer or Lionel Abrahams visited him during the day. Otherwise, I was the only man visiting a man dying of cancer, the only friend who knew.

Duggie went what he called 'stir-crazy'. He couldn't bear to be in the hospital. He desperately needed to get out. He began to fight with the staff. He refused the bed-pan and demanded to be taken to the toilets. He weakened, lost weight. His hair fell out as a result of the radium treatment. Without his dentures he looked like Gandhi. He seemed neglected, dirty. 'You see that fucken little bastard over there,' he indicated the legless old man two beds down. 'Tonight I'm going to get his neck in here,' indicating the crook of his knee, 'then I'm going to hold on,' he held his only foot with his only moving hand, 'and then I'll fucken well strangle him to death . . .' He nagged violently about the book. I said we could wait. He nagged Nadine and Lionel. They nagged me. I spoke to the doctor again. There was not much that he could say. The radium treatment would be effective only up to a certain point; thereafter, nothing more could be done. When that point was reached, Duggie would have to leave the hospital. Not enough beds. Where would he go? That became a case for the social workers – a familiar phrase in Duggie's life. I contacted a friend who ran a mission hospital in Zululand. When nothing more could be done for Duggie, would he take him in? He would be happy to help. I told Duggie that when he was well enough to travel, I would take him down to Zululand to recuperate. He wasn't particularly comforted. I began to despair of him ever finishing the book.

At that time, I was between jobs. I took a three-week excursion overseas to see what I could do with the book. I had it typed out virtually as it stood. Dugmore was threatening to leave the hospital. Where would he go? To friends in the township. What friends? Friends. Where were they now? Why didn't they come to visit? No answer. I begged him to wait until my return. He wept.

I left the book with an agent in London. I asked him to explain to the publishers that they should judge it by its best parts, that the rest would be improved upon. I even argued unfairly. I stressed how important to Dugmore a letter of interest would be. The book was accepted for this publication a year after Dugmore's death.

On my return, Duggie insisted on leaving the hospital immediately. Dr Selma Browde was the specialist who had administered his radium therapy at the General Hospital. He was at the end of his treatment. I consulted her and the doctor at Coronationville and was advised to wait a week or so before taking him down to Zululand. I saw Dugmore at Coronationville on a Wednesday, and promised to revisit him on the Friday. With a pig's knuckle. He said that he wouldn't be there. He wasn't. After his therapy at the General Hospital, he had had himself carried to a taxi and driven into the township. There was nothing to do but wait.

Then a week later, at my new job, a phone call. Dr Browde. Dugmore and his mother were at the General Hospital. (His mother! I had read about her death, questioned it, heard about it in detail.) She could no longer look after him, and had brought him back. The hospital would keep him until the end of the week. Then would I drive down to Zululand? I dashed up to the hospital and was taken to his ward. Dugmore was lying propped up in bed under a grey blanket. On his shiny bald head a knitted hat had slid askew. Beside him stood a little old woman, unquestionably his mother. He lay there like a snake with his one leg and lame arm. It was as if all his cancer was in his eyes. They were staring at me, phosphorescent.

His mother spoke. 'Mr Barney, I'm sorry, I've wanted to meet you often, but Duggie wouldn't let me. I wanted to meet you at Coronationville Hospital but he wouldn't let me. Me and my daughters used to visit him all the time there. I'm sorry, I couldn't look after him. I have to do the washing, Mr Barney, I have to look after the children. He was too heavy for me to lift, Mr Barney, I couldn't turn him over. And he was cursing all the time. I couldn't, Mr Barney; I'm too old, I'm too tired . . . I know he got money from you, Mr Barney, but he never gave me a penny . . .'

As she spoke, Duggie spoke in counterpoint, ignoring her words, acknowledging her as the old woman, never as his mother. 'All she has to do is make some black coffee . . . I came here just for some treatment . . . I won't stay . . . I'm going back . . .' All the time he spoke he stared at me. An open declaration. Now I knew the score. The lies. The cons. Those hospital trips to the 'loner'. Even the money for the old woman hadn't reached her. But he was there. On my back. For the rest of his life at least. At that moment I hated him. He hated me. I took the old woman out into the passage.

She spoke on. Duggie had always been a difficult child. He lost his leg at the age of eight. One day he came home screaming from a pain in his leg. The leg turned black; it had had to be amputated. He'd been to jail only twice to her knowledge. He'd never been up north in the army.

The following Saturday, after promising his mother that I would cover the cost of bringing his body back to Johannesburg, I drove Duggie down to Zululand. Lionel sat beside me. Duggie reclined among cushions and blankets in the back. It was a beautiful, gentle journey through the flat yellow landscapes each of us had a special feeling for. We all relaxed into an acceptance of the situation. At one point Duggie leaned back and said, 'You know, I'm really enjoying this drive.'

When we arrived at the mission hospital, he was skilfully settled between clean sheets and soft blue blankets in a ward of his own. It was there that the young nurse exclaimed, 'I know this man, I grew up under him . . . he used to play the guitar . . .' We left him radiant, a pile of manuscript paper beside his bed to encourage him to begin working again.

Parts of the book began to be published in newspapers. The first chapter was published by *London Magazine*. There were letters, clumsily typed.

Dear Barney
    First let me thank you for having brought me here. Otherwise Iwould have been dead by thistime.
    The treatment is ex celent everybod is so nice.
    Barrney, Iha tobe certain I haven't written a thing due to continuous headaches and a irritating pain inmy chest. The stuff is just orbiting in my brain wantigg to beplaced on paper. The Dr says I should take things easy for a while.
    PLEASE except this as a fact.
    NO JOKE.' BARNEY,
                XXXXIE. Whenare you coming? Barney can you organise a second hand battery shaver?
                BY,
                DUGGIE.
And BARNEY, PLEASE GET MESOME 'FIT' RELEAVING PILLS FROM Dr Broadie or Mr Tana.

Then, six weeks after taking Duggie to Zululand, a cable:
    'FEELING WORSE. COME FETCH IMMEDIATELY. DUGMORE.'
    I phoned hospitals in Johannesburg, tried doctors I knew. None would take him. I spoke to his mother. She couldn't possibly cope. It was pointless writing or phoning. I drove down with Lionel again.
    Duggie was delighted to see us. 'Good!' he said. 'When d'we leave?'
    'I'm sorry,' I said, 'I've driven here to tell you that you can't come back. Not yet.' I was still not to tell him that he had cancer.
    'You're taking me,' he said.
    'You are very sick. No hospital will take you in now. Your mother can't. You're being fed here, looked after, kept clean. Please, you must stay. When you're better, you can come back.'
    'You can't keep me here against my will . . .'
    We argued on and on, Lionel sitting silently by.
    'I'll get the police on to you,' Duggie threatened.

'Duggie, I can't take you.'

'I want to go back to Joburg.'

'Where? Where to in Joburg?'

'I don't care! Leave me in a gutter – I want to go back to Joburg.'

I knew what he meant. It was hard to argue.

'If I take you to your mother it will be hell in a week.'

'Take me to Joburg.' He started to weep. Then finally he said to Lionel, looking at me, 'I know why Barney doesn't want to take me back.' We both sat silent. 'He thinks I'm going to die.' We said nothing. We got up to go. Dugmore began to curse me. He threatened to have me arrested on a charge of abduction.

'I'll come again,' I said. He went on cursing me. We left. It seemed like the end of everything.

Before we left the mission, I said goodbye to the doctor in charge. He was very quiet and sympathetic. It seemed to me that he knew exactly what had happened, how final, how terrible this last interview had been. Lionel and I drove back to Johannesburg saying very little. I remember seeing some washerwomen, this time across a pale spring field, and, I think, watching them, that I learned something, changed a little. I remember wondering about Duggie, what remark he might have made or even yelled, seeing these women. He could have been passing, but he wasn't. The book might not have happened, but it did. Those papers beside his bed, his work, my work, might be burnt or blown away. These women would still be there in exactly the same way. But the world *would* be different without what we had attempted together. I never saw Duggie again.

Occasionally I received letters from people at the mission. They mentioned always that 'Dugmore would like to hear from his friends.' On each occasion, I phoned those of his friends I could and asked them to write. It was some weeks later, when I phoned the mission, that I discovered that the 'friends' included me. I was told that he spoke constantly of me. I promised to come down and see him over the weekend.

On the Friday they phoned me to say that Duggie was dead.

I contacted Duggie's family. I was working alone in the office that Saturday. His mother and his two sisters came swollen-eyed and weeping to see me there. We spoke about him for a while, exchanging anecdotes and even managing to laugh. Then they handed me the bill for the funeral. £107.10.0. A coffin for £75. I was stunned. My savings had been spent on the trip. I said it would be difficult.

A sister asked if I couldn't use some of the money from the story. Which story? The one that was sold overseas. I tried to explain that *London Magazine* had only paid £15. They were obviously not convinced. How much did they think it was? Duggie had said that he was going to get £150. I thought I would go crazy. I phoned the undertaker to ask the price of a good, strong, polished coffin. £25. That was how much I would contribute towards a coffin.

Duggie's youngest sister went with the undertaker's van to Zululand. I asked her to collect the manuscript for me. A few days later, she came to see me. She had a scab on her forehead. The van bringing Duggie back to Joburg had overturned and his face was bruised. She had collected the papers, but had left them in the township.

I went to Duggie's funeral with Lionel and an African friend. We didn't go to his mother's house, but straight to the cemetery. There was a heavy traffic of hearses, battered American cars and big rattling lorries coming and going. We found the grave, empty still. The cortège had not yet arrived. We sat in my car. The sun was white-hot. A long line of cars moved in and stopped nearby us. In a long, gleaming black hearse driven by a handsome young Indian was Duggie's coffin. Carved, trimmed in silver and covered with flowers. The £75 one.

Lionel and I were the only whites. A large crowd gathered around the grave. Duggie had a brother, too. The brother spoke. The preacher spoke. About Duggie's reverence. His goodness. There were several children there, weeping bitterly. I thought of the nurse in Zululand and the Duggie in her childhood and found myself close to weeping too. Then suddenly I was called upon to make a speech. I managed to grope through a few words.

We all went forward to drop earth on Duggie. As I bent, I looked down the four raw clay walls at his beautiful coffin. I thought of his dream of Freeman shoes when only one foot really knew the difference. The coffin was the same. I felt ashamed for having argued.

Afterwards, I went to shake hands with Duggie's mother.

There was a tension. I tried to mention the manuscript papers to his sister. She looked blank. As we began to get into my car, a young man came up to me. He was asking, he said, for the family, about the money from Duggie's writing that was sold in London. I repeated my story. I showed him a letter from London. Car doors were slamming all around. There was dust. It was too hot. I just stopped talking. This was Duggie's final con. I knew that it would be a long time before I got the papers back. It was.

Barney Simon
Johannesbury 1989

Books from

FOUR WALLS EIGHT WINDOWS

Algren, Nelson.
Never Come Morning. pb: $7.95

Anderson, Sherwood.
The Triumph of the Egg. pb: $8.95

Boetie, Dugmore.
Familiarity Is the Kingdom of the Lost. pb: $6.95

Brodsky, Michael.
X in Paris. pb: $9.95

Brodsky, Michael.
Xman. cl: $21.95, pb: $11.95

Codrescu, Andrei, ed.
American Poetry Since 1970: Up Late. pb. $14.95

David, Kati.
A Child's War: World War II Through the Eyes of Children. cl: $17.95

Dubuffet, Jean.
Asphyxiating Culture and Other Writings. cl: $17.95

Howard-Howard, Margo (with Abbe Michaels).
I Was a White Slave in Harlem. pb: $12.95

Johnson, Phyllis, and Martin, David, eds.
Frontline Southern Africa: Destructive Engagement. cl: $23.95 pb: $14.95

Null, Gary.
The Egg Project: Gary Null's Guide to Good Eating. cl: $21.95, pb: $12.95

Santos, Rosario, ed.
**And We Sold the Rain: Contemporary Fiction from Central America.
cl: $18.95, pb: $9.95**

Schultz, John.
No One Was Killed. pb: $9.95

Sokolov, Sasha.
A School for Fools. pb: $9.95

Wasserman, Harvey.
Harvey Wasserman's History of the United States. pb: $6.95

Weber, Brom, ed.
**O My Land, My Friends: The Selected Letters of Hart Crane.
cl: $21.95, pb: $12.95**

Zerden, Sheldon.
The Best of Health. cl:$23.95, pb $12.95

To order, send check or money order to Four Walls Eight Windows, P.O. Box 548, Village Station, New York, N.Y. 10014, or call 1-800-835-2246, ext. 123. Add $2.50 postage and handling for the first book and 50¢ for each additional book.